LITTLE SNOWMAN
BASEBALL

Jake Snow

Don't expect to find anything fancy on these pages.

I'm simply here to deliver a series of thoughts, ideas, observations, and memories regarding the lives of hundreds of millions of people who have been touched by Little League baseball, in any number of different capacities.

But specifically, my points of emphasis will be focused on two individual characters who have been dominating the culture of Little Leagues across the world for more than seventy-five years.

Their names are easy to remember—Ace and Ace Junior. It isn't gonna be hard to follow the bouncing ball here.

Ace is the name I'll commonly use when referring generically to a Little League coach.

Ace Junior will be the name I'll commonly use when referring generically to a Little League coach's son.

You won't have any trouble differentiating between the two of them because their roles in these stories will be crystal clear. Sadly, they will be as easy to recognize as somebody with two noses on their face.

Unfortunately.

Here's something that could have happened to any one of us while we were growing up.

You're nine years old.

You've been taught many things, *"Don't talk to strangers"*, "Make sure you wait for the white Walk sign before you Cross the Street", "Look Both Ways", Always say Please and Thank You", "Respect your Elders", "Wipe your feet when you come into the house", "Always wear clean underwear", and hundreds more.

You might be little, but you're learning an awful lotta stuff.

You live about a block and a half from a convenience store, but you've never gone there all by yourself yet. Between your house and the store, there's an intersection with a crosswalk and a traffic light.

One night, your mom is busy cooking supper and realizes that she needs a gallon of milk. She asks if you feel ready to go by yourself to get it for her.

She quickly goes over the rules again and you're off on your maiden solo voyage. No more holding hands!

When you get down to the corner, there's a couple of high school kids crossing the street and the *Walk* sign is white, so it's OK to go because you looked both ways.

It's clear sailing. All systems go!

You buy the gallon of milk and take your change. And now it's time to head back home.

You get to the intersection and push the pedestrian button on the pole. There are cars going up and down both sides of the street for a few minutes, but it sure seems like it's taking a lot longer than usual for the *Walk* sign to come on.

Meanwhile the red *Don't Walk* sign just stays lit.

And what you don't realize, and have absolutely no way of knowing, is that the *Walk* sign on that side of the street is broken, and it's never going to change colors until the Public Works Department shows up to fix it.

You sure didn't expect to have to wait so long.

And, oh by the way, did you know that a gallon of milk weighs eight and a half pounds?

And those eight and a half pounds definitely present a problem when you only weigh about sixty pounds yourself!

Yeah, it's getting pretty heavy, but you don't want to set the milk down on the ground, so you try to hang tough.

A few more minutes pass by, and now you need to go to the bathroom. And you're not sure how long you are gonna be able to hold it either. You are hopping on one leg and then the other.

You're worried that you might even wet your pants.

You don't have a cell phone because your dad said you're not old enough yet. You are incommunicado.

The *Don't Walk sign* is still lit, so you go back and push the button a whole bunch more times, because you wonder if you hadn't pushed it hard enough the first time.

There is no fun going on at all.

 It's horrible.

What are his options?

What could he do?

Now ask yourself, what would YOU have done if you'd been faced with the same set of circumstances as a nine-year-old?

Alright—now let's take the same kid, same age, same rules.

His dad signs him up for Little League and the little guy is thrilled. He can't wait until he can practice with his team, and play in his first game. He's been watching baseball for years.

He's so excited that somebody is going to teach him how to play.

Finally the big day arrives! It's time to practice and meet his teammates. And they're all going to start playing baseball together.

Two weeks later, the team is ready for its first game!

They gave the boy an orange jersey with the name of his team on the front with a baseball cap to match. Once he got them, he stood in front of a mirror for hours, posing with his bat and the new glove that his dad bought him for the season.

He's as happy as a little kid could possibly be.

The game starts, but he doesn't get to play in the first inning. Almost all of the other kids got the chance to run out onto the field and play.

But Ace made him sit on the bench, and eyeball the proceedings from there. He'd have to wait for his turn.

He watches almost the whole game from the dugout.

In the last inning, Ace sends him out to right field. The youngster runs out there as fast as he could go. It's finally his chance to play!

Nobody hits the ball to him, but he's in fielding position and ready for anything that might come his way.

When his team comes up to bat in the last inning, he's bursting with joy because he's finally going to get his first time at bat. But before he can hit, the third out is made and he doesn't get to swing the bat that day.

It happens over and over again. Most games he gets to bat, but usually not more than once.

He wants to play more, of course, but he figures the coach doesn't think he's good enough.

Put yourself into his shoes again. What are his options this time around?

What could he do?

What would the nine-year-old YOU have been able to do?

And you might be wondering why that one little kid had to sit on the bench for five innings, while most of his teammates were on the field playing baseball.

It's because Ace elected to banish him to that bench, and keep him there until it was absolutely necessary to send him into the game!

As mindless as it sounds, Ace is gonna display the same type of nonsense tonight in Anniston and Nottingham and Ocean City and Muskogee and Zanesville...

I believe that if I didn't write these particular words, in my own inimitable folksy style, nothing would ever change, and an extremely disturbing status quo would continue on until the end of time.

These ideas can't be properly conveyed in just a couple of paragraphs, and that's why I decided to write an entire volume on this subject.

But whenever I do get a chance to speak in person, with anyone who's ever been touched by Little League baseball, it only takes me a moment to get my point across cheerfully, comfortably, and powerfully.

Believe it or don't—I'm involved in more than 18,000 one-on-one, face-to-face conversations every single year. And they happen in one of the most festive environments in the world—the Las Vegas Strip.

The atmosphere features an enormous amount of people who are in town on vacation and ready to let loose!

So I head out onto Las Vegas Boulevard and meet those tourists every morning of the year. And I don't leave until I've shared my thoughts with fifty brand-new friends.

How do I know that they feel the same way about me? I know because they actually write their names down in my journal. Whether they are my first daily entry, or my 50th, they all agree with my views on how to properly coach Little League baseball.

It's the coolest darn thing too, because every one of these encounters is completely random. People come from all over creation to visit us. More than 42 million people came to see us last year! *Allow that to percolate for a minute.*

And my new friends realize immediately that I'm extremely serious about what I'm doing, and why I'm doing it. In two shakes of a lamb's tail, they're able to look into my eyes and understand just how important this is to me —and to them!

Although we may have met for just a few fleeting moments in time, we can remain *friends* for a lifetime. They will never forget me.

Whenever they think of Little League baseball, they will think of me.

"I've learned that people will forget what you said, people will forget what you did, but people will never forget how you made them feel."- Maya Angelou

You don't meet people very often who possess the incredible amount of passion that I can exhibit from one minute to the next. It's one of the greatest gifts that I've been given, and I will be forever grateful for it.

I simply share a few highlights with my new buddies, who have now become my comrades, and they promise me that they will read and share *Little Snowman Baseball.*

And my outreach doesn't end out on Las Vegas Boulevard either.

When afternoon rolls around, I start dialing my telephone, and I don't stop until I've spoken to a young lady real estate agent in each of our fifty states.

And I'm doing this on Easter and Christmas and Thanksgiving and New Year's and Halloween and July 4th and Groundhog's Day. I'm sure that I've driven home the point.

No days off.

The only disclaimer is that I do make a three-day odyssey to *Cedar Point Roller Coaster Park* in Sandusky, Ohio every August.

But my adventurous summer getaway just means that I talk with hundreds of people at Cedar Point, in the restaurants, at the airports, and any other place I might go.

When it's all tallied up, I personally touch more than 36,000 people every year. And I ask every single one of them to tell their friends and family about *Little Snowman Baseball*.

If you've ever watched a baseball game when the Boston Red Sox are playing a home game, it's almost always a sellout crowd at Fenway Park—which just so happens to have a seating capacity of 36,000 people.

Sound familiar?

This means that, with just my regular daily personal outreach efforts, it would give me the chance to have a conversation with every single one of those Fenway fans during the course of just one calendar year!

What we are fixing together is not just a dirty little secret—it's filthy, and it's grimy. It's a nasty version of an *Ol' Boys Network* that's gone unspoken, and unchecked, for nearly a hundred years.

I'm doing everything I can to stop this behavior in its tracks.

And you can add this as a virtual certainty. I want you to proceed with the knowledge that I don't care one bit whether people like me or not.

This is not a popularity contest.

Bottom line: This needs to stop immediately, and I would love to energize you—and deputize you—so you can become an important member of this world-wide solution with me.

I'm also not here seeking to win a Pulitzer Prize.

My writing style, and its content, is probably not gonna be one that's familiar to most of you. If you're an English teacher, or a fact checker, this might not be the place for you.

I've got a lot of things to say and, trust me, I'm going to say them my way!

I can vividly remember a time when a Congressman called me a *journalist* while he was introducing me to speak at a banquet.

But I am not a *journalist*, nor have I ever been one. I've never allowed myself to be constrained by any expected behavior, or societal norms.

You should have seen all those little Catholic nuns running around trying to tame me during my thirteen colorful school years that took place under their tutelage. They had no chance! Grin.

I do whatever I want, whenever I want. My behavior is not difficult to decipher.

I even acted however I wanted when I was in the Navy. And the Army. And the Air Force. Yes, all three!

Laugh all you want, but I've got stories to tell about a few military personnel who did try to order me around from time to time— Sergeants, Chiefs, Colonels and Admirals—but their efforts usually landed on deaf ears.

In reality, I have always created an environment where nobody would have any reason to tell me what to do. Either I had already done it, or I was the guy in charge of getting it done.

Conducting myself with this level of confidence can be traced back to when a teacher gave me an assignment to do a book report about the *State of Vermont,* when I was in fourth grade.

I found *Vermont,* in the 1960 edition of the Encyclopedia Americana, and its description began with this quote,

"A Vermonter will do almost anything you ask him to do and nearly nothing that you tell him to do."

Bullseye!

I lived in Vermont, so I must have been a Vermonter. Am I right? Grin. And I was in sync with every word contained in that quote. Then I conditioned myself to behave that way every day, ever since.

Recently, I thought about how I have visited all four corners of the earth, and not one person has ever disagreed with me on this topic. And, as I've already told you, I've personally communicated with hundreds of thousands of people along my life's journey.

Count yourself among them, and please help me to create and enjoy these positive changes that are taking place nightly, all over the world!

I've planned on leading the charge on this for more than twenty-five years, and I am ever so grateful for every one of you who boards this train with me.

Thanks so much for being there!

I've put together a little quiz to help illustrate the reasons that Ace—and his like-minded buddies—need to be watched very closely.

HEY ACE:

- Does Ace Junior play every inning of every game?
- Are there other kids who play fewer innings than Junior plays?

- Do you have an uncanny ability to spot athletic talent?
- Do you sometimes feel as if you are outwitting the coach in the other dugout?
- Did you score high marks on your Little League Coaching Exam? *This one throws them off a bit when they realize that there is no Little League Coaching Exam.*
- Is Ace Junior on your pitching staff?
- Does he play shortstop when he is not pitching?
- Are there players on your team who have never pitched or played shortstop?
- Are you on the cutting edge of scouting, analytics, and player development?
- Does Ace Junior bat in one of the first four spots in the batting order, in EVERY game?
- Are there other kids who've never batted in any of those top four spots in the line-up, in ANY game?
- Can my kid come over to your house and watch Ace Junior go through his rigorous pre-game training regimen?
- Do you spend time at night poring over the statistics in your scorebooks?
- Do you plan special strategies for upcoming games?
- Have you ever had one kid pinch-hit for another kid, in order to gain a competitive advantage?
- Have you ever had an argument with a Little League umpire?

Spend a moment or two considering your answers. My responses to these questions will be displayed liberally throughout this volume.

I remember playing in my first game as a kid. And it will forever rank right at the top of my favorite lifetime highlights.

Everything was fresh and new. And, it was so exciting! I'd been waiting for years to experience my first official game!

Our team had practiced a few times, but I still didn't know if I was going to start the game, or come off the bench. I wondered what position I'd be playing, and where I'd be batting in the lineup.

I had no idea.

And I was completely at the coach's mercy, wasn't I?

He could have put me wherever he wanted. I was only nine years old, but I'd spent the past two summers playing in pick-up games with kids who were several grades ahead of me in school.

And the more I played, the better I got. It turned out that I was just as good, or better, than any of them.

I was more than ready to play. It was my first taste of organized baseball, and I was so pumped!

But that coach, who began reading the lineup card, was the sole focus in my world. He held the hammer.

And then, the very first words that came out of his mouth were magical, and never to be forgotten,

"Snowman, you're catching and batting leadoff..."

It was the first time anybody had ever called me by my last name. They never did that in school, or at home. Not only did he call me by my last name, but he added a nickname—SNOWMAN!—that has stood the test of time ever since that day.

Nobody had ever called me a catcher either. And there'd be a darn good reason for that. I'd never been a catcher before, not even in practice.

I was going to be strapping on the tools of *ignorance*, as catcher's equipment is affectionately known, and I had no idea how to even put the stuff on!

Apparently, the coach also thought that I was good enough to be our team's first batter of the season too!

Let's get this show on the road!

I'd already developed instincts and reflexes far beyond normal expectations. I made myself better at baseball every day since I was four years old.

That included playing thousands of games all by myself. Some of them were outside in the yard, some were while bouncing off the walls in my bedroom, and countless more played out in the theater of my mind.

All baseball, all the time!

My goal in life was to play left field for the Boston Red Sox, and I was already getting a chance to play catcher on a tiny baseball field in Northern Vermont!

And I was gonna get to be the first batter of the game too! The first batter of the season!

Holy Smokes!

The majority of you will be able to clearly understand what I am trying to accomplish in the early stages of this volume.

None of this will be difficult to comprehend.

I'll be very convincing when I prove to you how badly our Little Leagues are broken. Next, I'll provide a rock-solid simple solution.

And then we will fix this together. One coach at a time.

Once this information hits its target, rarely does anyone put up even one ounce of resistance. Yet there will always be those who refuse to change their minds, no matter what they learn.

Sadly, there are coaches who are so *dug-in,* with their hard and fast stances, that they'll fight like the dickens for the right to continue displaying the same ugly behavior they've been featuring for far too long already.

One fact is unmistakable, there isn't a coach on earth who could read this entire volume and not modify their behavior afterward.

Offering these thoughts, from many different angles and viewpoints, has proven to be the most effective strategy to create these amazing shifts in beliefs and attitudes.

From playing to watching to coaching to cheering, almost every family has been touched by Little League baseball in one form or fashion.

And those *touches* can be remembered in any number of different ways.

In millions of homes, Little League memories are fond and pleasant. These families remember that it was a time for great plays and home runs and All-Star teams and championship trophies and ice cream after the games!

Yet the narrative is considerably different in millions of other households. These families don't recall their Little League days to be happy ones at all.

Far too many kids never got a chance to play very much baseball. For those little guys, their own coach chose to put them on the bench, instead of on the field.

Those kids have absolutely no reason to look back and feel any pleasure associated with their days in Little League.

They wanted to play baseball. So they signed up to play baseball. And Ace prevented them from playing baseball!

At the same time, Ace had a son on the team, and Ace Junior never sat on the bench all season. Not even once.

It's just as simple as that. This happens on every single team in the history of Little League. The coach puts his kid on the field for the whole game, every game.

Then he takes another guy's kid, and puts him on the bench to watch the game, every game.

And it happens on every team, in every league, every night, everywhere!

Frankly, Little League coaches can't quite seem to understand that their mighty offspring will rarely benefit from the nepotism they display, night after night, year after year.

Ace conducts himself in a way that he believes to be proper. He copies what he's seen before. He's the Commander-in-Chief.

His goal is to win those championships.

But with his sole focus on those coveted trophies, he winds up operating totally oblivious to the fact that he's completely out of touch with any semblance of reality.

All it takes for us to win this battle is to create a newfound awareness that can penetrate Ace's thick skull.

Once we've gotten his attention, he'll be able to tweak his methods immediately, with a transition so seamlessly smooth that nobody will even notice!

Ace's wrongful behavior would continue forever if somebody doesn't intervene and force a change.

It's not unusual for people to resist new methods and ideas. When something is foreign at first, it's very likely going to be met with stiff opposition.

This is no different. Except for one thing, there is no opposition to what I am saying here!

But if nobody pipes up and says anything, the status quo is all that will remain.

Somebody has to do something about this, and that somebody is me. And YOU!

"Nothing happens until something moves. „

Jackie Gee was the morning DJ on WFQP Radio

He had the highest-rated show in the region, which helped to make him a local celebrity who was easily recognizable all around the town.

In addition to his morning show, Jackie hosted an extremely popular *Oldies Party on Saturday nights.*

Arnie Adams was a high school kid who lived just a few blocks from the radio station. Arnie spent all of his free time practicing to be a disc jockey.

He wanted to follow in the footsteps of Jackie Gee. Arnie looked up to Jackie with reverence.

During his senior year, Arnie mustered up the courage to approach Jackie Gee at the radio station. He dressed up in his best duds, then he walked in and asked to speak with his idol.

Jackie came out and greeted him and he told Arnie to go downstairs to the production studio and put together an *air check.* He said that he'd come down and listen to it in a little while.

Arnie's heart leapt! He was talking to the man who was a giant in his world. And he was going to get a chance to show Jackie Gee exactly what he'd learned during thousands of hours of practice.

It was 9:30 in the morning when Arnie went into that studio. He spent more than an hour getting his presentation just the way he knew that Jackie would like it.

But what Arnie didn't know was that Jackie Gee had left the radio station at ten o'clock and went out to play golf.

Arnie waited in that production studio for more than six hours, but Jackie Gee never came back.

He left what he'd been working on with the receptionist and went home. He waited for two weeks to hear from Jackie. But he never did.

So he decided to call the station to see if he could get some feedback.

Jackie picked up the phone and told Arnie that he still hadn't found the time to review his work yet, but then asked, *"Do you have a truck by any chance?"* Arnie didn't have one, but he knew he could borrow one.

Jackie told him that a band was coming into town and that it would be a big feather in his cap if he could go and meet them at the airport to help bring some of their gear to the radio station.

Arnie borrowed his friend's truck and went to pick up the band.

It was going to be his first chance to hang out with the guys at the station. Plus there was gonna be a jam session and a catered buffet.

Arnie was thrilled and eager to be part of those activities.

Then he noticed Jackie Gee standing in the doorway motioning for him to come into his office.

Arnie went in and Jackie thanked him, and then gave him a five-dollar-bill for gas. Jackie said that he'd listen to Arnie's tape and give him some feedback very soon.

He walked Arnie down to the reception area and said goodnight to him.

No mingling. No buffet. No feedback. No nothing. And Jackie never called him.

Never.

Jackie and Arnie would never meet again.

Well, actually they did reunite sixteen years later.

That's when Arnie Adams walked into radio station KRVY, as their new General Manager and Program Director.

And guess who was the morning DJ at KRVY? Jackie Gee!

Arnie Adams was Jackie Gee's new boss. Karma? You tell me!

It ain't as much fun when the rabbit's got the gun!

Arnie let Jackie twist in the wind for a couple weeks.

Then one Tuesday morning, Arnie summoned Jackie into his office and handed him a five-dollar-bill.

And he walked Jackie to the exit.

No buffets. No jam sessions. No discussion. Bye-Bye Jackie!

If my coach had been Jackie Gee, my life may have gone in a totally different direction.

Think about it. My coach had power that was absolute. Whatever he considered to be the right way to coach was the way it was going to be.

Had he simply overlooked me and made me sit on the bench all the time, it would have been devastating. And it wouldn't have even crossed his mind what might have been going on inside my little head.

I LOVED the game of baseball.

I played it for hours every day. Rain or shine. I'd throw my red rubber ball against my aunt's house continuously. My defense was years ahead of schedule.

Every weekend, Dad took me for batting practice at the park. I learned to clobber the baseball.

I thought about the game day and night. I became a baseball fanatic. I learned the game. I knew the rules.

My size could have worked against me too. I was tiny, the

smallest guy on the team. But I'm sure that never even entered my consciousness. As far as I was concerned, I was a big leaguer wearing a Little Leaguer's uniform.

That man, and I can't even remember his name, could have changed my destiny forever.

Thankfully he didn't, but way too many coaches, in far too many places, have used their iron fists to pulverize the hopes and dreams of millions of little kids.

Millions.

The scary part is that Ace—and his henchmen—are completely oblivious to the damage they have been doing.

These words cannot be discarded without consideration.

We certainly need winners and losers in all of our games. The kids need to have a chance to experience the joys and heartbreaks that come with winning and losing.

But for that to happen, they all must have a chance to play.

Every single one of them.

Take me to the Library, I'm sixty years overdue!

Imagine the late fees!

I have a clear understanding of what's necessary to powerfully convey these principles and ideals. It's my wild passion accompanying a single-minded purpose.

This isn't my story!

This one belongs to all of us, and we're creating major positive changes because it only takes the tiniest of tweaks to make this work for us.

I don't seek more riches, I seek more wisdom.

"Are you Jake Snow?"

I didn't recognize the pretty young woman who'd just marched right up, and looked me squarely in my eyes.

I smiled and replied, "*Yes, I'm Jake.*"

"*Well, I just wanted to let you know that my son quit playing baseball because of you.*"

"*I'm sorry to hear that. What's his name?*"

"*His name is Ronnie Watkins.*"

"*Wow, I thought that Ronnie really enjoyed himself when he was playing baseball with us that season.*"

"*Yes, he most certainly did*", she laughed, "*He loved every minute of that season! The problem was when you stopped coaching and he came out ready to play again the next year.*"

"*He thought that all coaches were going to be like you and he quit right after the second practice because his coach wasn't anything like you at all!*"

And she's right, there's nobody else like me. Naturally, it follows that there is nobody else like you either.

We're all different. No two snowflakes are alike.

I've spoken to a lot of people about the way I believe the environment should be structured when little kids are being coached.

I demand that all kids are to be treated fairly and responsibly by those who are in a position of authority.

I've got every credential someone would ever need to offer these thoughts and opinions with credibility. I've played, coached, parented, umpired, written, and broadcasted sports ever since I was a preschooler.

I've also had many people tell me stories about their experiences and memories from Little League.

I've seen, or played in, tens of thousands of games from the pee wees to the major leagues. I love my game and want it to be equally accessible for every kid that wants to play.

If just one kid gets an opportunity to play, when he didn't have the chance to play previously, I am winning!

But my goals are much loftier than that. This isn't about just one kid. It's about all kids.

I write stories about baseball every day of my life. This story is a bit longer, and it's gonna be available for consumption until the end of time.

That's the neat thing about books and the people who write

them. I could be six feet under the ground, playing baseball every day in Snowball Heaven, while you're reading about our Little Snowman.

Written words will always outlast their authors. They're something we leave behind. And I contend that the information shared here today will be valid forever and a year. There is no expiration date on any of this.

What you'll find here are nothing more than common sense ideas being put down in writing for the first time. More than sixty years of watching Little League coaches make the same terrible, head-scratching decisions continues to anger and disappoint me.

My methodology and ideology are easy to understand, even easier to apply!

And I've pushed all my chips into the middle of the table because I'm intent on fixing something that absolutely needs to be corrected!

Every kid who signs up to play should be treated in a way that gives him an equal chance at cracking a solid base hit or making a good catch or firing a nice, crisp fastball toward home plate.

But too many kids never get a chance to do any of those things

21

and their entire experience ends up lasting just a few practices or one short year.

Every one of these kids is special. Any one of them could be a budding baseball superstar. But we will never know their potential unless they are given a chance to play and prove themselves.

I don't care if the kid can't throw the ball five feet on the first day. I know that if you work with him, he'd be able to throw it ten times that far by the end of the first week.

Everybody has a story to tell about when they were a part of the Little League landscape. And far too often, those stories reveal a frustration that continues on as a sour taste in their mouths throughout their lifetimes.

Having to sit on the bench in Little League creates an inner narrative that is simply untrue.

I once met a wise man who shared some great advice with me.

He told me to make my readers understand the problem, and then solve it for them.

And solve it I have!

With gentleness, love and leverage, these words are spreading to every city, town, and hamlet—freely, purposefully, and powerfully!

The best part is that *The Good Guys Are Gonna Win in the End!*

Little Snowman Baseball wouldn't be nearly as effective if I began a conversation by telling Ace that he was doing something wrong.

There is no question that Ace is acting recklessly and foolishly, but the mere notion that he might be complicit in any wrong-doing never even entered his consciousness.

Ace would become defensive right away and wouldn't be the least bit receptive to any new ideas that might help him realize that he should re-examine his coaching style.

Before meeting me, or coming into contact with my words, Ace believes that he is the fuel that starts the engine and keeps it purring right along.

Further, he knows that Ace Junior is the main cog in the wheel of a team that's on a collision course with the league championship.

But fresh and enlightened behaviors are beginning to surface. And Aces from all around the world have begun changing their ways immediately after they've been introduced to these ideas for the very first time.

And once he's been exposed to Little Snowman Baseball, Ace will understand that he's been doing dastardly things to little kids.

Now Ace can take this newly acquired knowledge and be able to show people what he's learned in Bethlehem and Odessa and Ventura and Lakewood and Quincy...

Chicks dig the long ball every bit as much as we love hitting them.

Now let's allow our minds to wander to the kid who never got a chance to play so he never got a chance to hit the long ball, or even the short ball.

It's a shame when that occurs.

I didn't let that happen when I coached. They all played and they all sat on the bench. I was an equal opportunity coach. Every single one of them played lots of baseball.

All the players on my team played the same amount of baseball as every one of their teammates.

The way I had it figured was that if they were on my baseball team, they must have wanted to play baseball. So I let them play baseball. All of them.

Seemed reasonable to me.

I agreed to coach, but just for one season.

I began the year not knowing one darn thing about the administrative part of the job. For instance, I didn't have a clue as to how the rosters were assembled.

My guess was that somebody in the league office would divide up the names, and then give each coach a roster with their list of little ballplayers.

Nope, I was wrong! I couldn't have been more wrong.

When I called to ask, the lady told me that the tryouts were going to be on Saturday morning and then we'd be conducting a Player Draft on Sunday night!

Huh?

We were going to draft ten and eleven-year-old kids?!

Yup, we were supposed to bring clipboards to the tryouts and chart the level of talent for each player so we could later draft specific kids onto our teams!

Are you kidding me?

Kids, some of them who are still doing flash cards in math class, would be subjected to a draft as if these ever-so-shrewd Little League coaches—and their staffs!—would be able to deduce the power, strength, speed, stamina, dedication, passion, and potential of each youngster!

I did go over to watch those tryouts that Saturday morning, but I didn't bring a clipboard. I brought a coffee instead. I didn't write anything down either.

Every Snow Often, I'd see little groups of two or three men, talking in hushed voices, while plotting their strategies. Ridiculous as it seemed to me, this is how these leagues are set up and these guys were playing to win.

I went to that draft and the behavior I witnessed there was disgraceful.

It didn't take long before a big argument broke out, and loud angry voices came to the forefront of everybody's consciousness,

"You picked first LAST YEAR! He's gotta be on my team! His dad is my new assistant coach! He has to be on MY roster! Now how do you like getting a dose of your own medicine?!!!"

It had all the elements of a war room. What was developing in front of me was pretty darn scary.

In the second round, I chose an eleven-year-old who I'd never seen or heard of in my life. My choice was completely random.

And the guy directly across the table from me went ballistic,

"I KNEW you were going to take him! I knew it!!! I've had my eye on him since November, and here you go stealing him right out from under my nose!"

And tears ran down the guy's cheeks. I only tell you this because you can't make this stuff up.

That's when I stood up and made what I thought was a pretty fair proclamation,

"Look, this one here on the list is my son. He'll play for me. As far as all of the other kids on my roster, if you want them, they are all yours. Just give me a bunch of kids that want to play baseball. And any players that you don't want, I'll be happy to take them too."

Then I sat down. Everybody looked at me as if I had just landed in a space ship from *Planet Nutjob.*

And it became further alarming when those guys took me up on my offer right away, and not just one or two of them either. They raided my roster like vultures and never blinked an eye!

My views on the first day that I began to coach were the same ones I had on the final day I coached. I felt as if my job boiled down to teaching them the game as best I could, by showing them how to be good players, good teammates, and good friends.

Does that sound crazy to you?

Sadly, that Draft Night craziness is rampant in Schenectady and Yuma and Kyoto and Maple Grove and Joliet...

"How would you like to be a leftover?"

Comedian George Carlin asked that question during one of his stand-up comedy routines and then he stayed silent, for a pregnant pause, in order to let his question marinate for the audience.

Then he said," *Well, I guess being a leftover wouldn't be so bad if they were taking people out to be shot!"*

It made perfect sense to me. All of us want to be included in the activities we enjoy and it hurts like the dickens when we get left out against our wishes.

Do you think that a *leftover* and a *benchwarmer* are the exact same thing?

Some of you may know bits and pieces of the Eddie Gaedel story.

On August 19, 1951, Gaedel stepped up to the plate for the St. Louis Browns against the Detroit Tigers as the leadoff batter in the second game of a doubleheader.

Wearing the number 1/8 on the back of his uniform—yes, a fraction!—Eddie earned a *walk* because the pitcher missed the strike zone with all four of his pitches.

So Eddie Gaedel trotted on down to first base. Then he was immediately removed from the game, being replaced by a pinch-runner, and Eddie went back to the dugout.

It was Gaedel's major league debut but, once he left the field that day, Eddie would never play baseball again.

The reason for that was because Eddie Gaedel wasn't a *real* major league baseball player. In fact, he wasn't a baseball player at all.

Everything about his appearance in that big-league game that afternoon was nothing more than a publicity stunt. It was orchestrated by an owner, Bill Veeck, who was trying to put some additional fans in his grandstands.

You see, Eddie Gaedel was a circus midget that Veeck recruited in an effort to create a little buzz for a big league ballclub that was floundering in last place in the league standings.

Veeck's idea was to illustrate that a batter who stood only three feet six inches tall, even shorter when he was crouching down, would make it darn near impossible for a pitcher to have the precision necessary to throw any strikes.

Eddie proved his owner's point during his one turn at bat that afternoon. The pitcher really didn't even come close on any one of his pitches, so Gaedel did indeed get his walk and then made his way down to first base triumphantly!

And that should have been the end of the Eddie Gaedel story.

Sadly, it wasn't.

Eddie Gaedel's legend has lived on in a most unusual and disturbing way.

Since that fateful day, Little League coaches have employed a similar strategy by taking their smallest players and have them crouch down in the exact same way that little Eddie Gaedel did back in 1951.

As a young boy runs up to bat, Ace stops him near the on-deck circle. The kid is instructed to crouch down as low as he possibly can in an attempt to coax a walk from the pitcher.

Unfortunately, it works every time. So Ace uses this supposed *cutting-edge technology* as a new weapon in his arsenal.

Some of the little guys are even told to crouch down like that every single time they come to bat for the entire season!

It's crazy, and its widespread, and it needs to be stopped right now.

It naturally raises the question as to how much baseball this little guy is actually getting to play when he is told to do that repeatedly.

And why does the kid usually quit playing after just one year of Little League?

Why wouldn't he quit? Wouldn't you?

The youngster leaves the game behind because he is convinced that he isn't any good at baseball. Ace has reinforced that incorrect mindset all season long.

So for the remainder of the kid's life, he believes in his heart that he didn't even belong on his own Little League baseball team.

The problem lies in the fact that our little buddy might have been the best player on the whole team! How would anyone ever know? After all, he was only ten years old.

Ace determined that the young boy wasn't good enough to compete with his teammates, and then reduced him to the same role Eddie Gaedel played in the 1950s!

My point is simple. When any kid plays Little League baseball, how in the heck do you think that you know what his ability level is unless you give him a chance to swing that bat or throw that pitch?

That kid could be Babe Ruth, for crying out loud!

And there are potential Babe Ruth's in Moline and Lake Charles and Clarksburg and Tallahassee and Bismarck...

We are all born to do something in this world. Many of us find it. Others never seem to figure it out.

When Michael Jordan, perhaps the greatest basketball player ever to lace up a pair of sneakers, stepped up to the podium to deliver his NBA Hall of Fame induction speech, he spent considerable time lamenting the fact that he had been cut from his high school basketball team.

I say again for possible penetration:

Michael Jordan was supposedly NOT good enough to play high school basketball according to the coach who made that decision!

Obviously, Michael hadn't forgotten about how much that decision stung him.

And as if that wasn't bad enough with Michael Jordan, the Varsity basketball coach for Hall of Famer Shaquille O'Neal cut him from the high school squad too!

Unbelievable!

This may appear to be apples and oranges, but it most certainly is not!

If those high school coaches, who were paid employees with actual credentials who interviewed and competed for the position, could make those inexplicably horrendous decisions on two of the top ten players ever to play in the NBA, how could it possibly hold true that Ace wouldn't make the same mistakes with a ten-year-old getting his first opportunity to play the game?

I'm definitely seeking to change people's beliefs and behaviors. I make no bones about it.

I know that I have written enough well-chosen words, with a fire-breathing passion, to make people realize that the ways that they've previously seen, and copied, are not even close to being the right way to handle these coaching responsibilities.

It's so cool when I am able to put *Little Snowman Baseball* into the hands of parents, and other interested parties, who can then share it with a coach that they can see is operating without a clue.

The Little League coaching gig should have nothing to do with clearing mantel space for shiny new trophies to display!

The coaches who really concern me are the ones who believe that Ace Junior is the centerpiece of the team and the rest of the kids are merely pawns in their master plans!

I'll tell you right now that if there are ten teams in your league, there are eight or nine coaches who feel exactly this way.

Just sayin'...

They'll frighten you with their thoughts and beliefs in Lubbock and Kennebunkport and Waterloo and Hershey and Anaheim...

This may be the most important baseball book in history.

Who would make such an outlandish claim?

Surely it's a mighty high standard to achieve, but this volume contains heaps and gobs of wisdom and plenty of food for thought.

I tell stories that help to illustrate my positions, and voice my displeasure, about the way that Little League coaching has destroyed the hopes and dreams of so many youngsters from all around the world.

I present this material to you in a manner that is very unsophisticated, mainly because I am not sophisticated in the least.

Besides, I don't need to be suave and debonair in order to make sure that this information is distributed to new coaches every day of the year.

It is spreading like wildfire.

In its highest and most polished form, baseball is played by men who earn millions of dollars. And every one of those players started out as a little kid who had to learn how to play.

What if you were the person who stood in the way of a little boy who just wanted a chance to play the game of baseball?

Would that make you feel like a big man?

I only ask that because Ace stands in their way every night in Walnut Grove and Key West and Princeville and Bellevue and Livingston...

You can't take a cookie cutter and make all of your little players behave the same way.

If you have more than one child, you know exactly what I mean.

I really enjoyed teaching my Little Leaguers about discipline and reminding them that we were all part of a team. They were equally responsible to follow the rules and be respectful.

One day, a young man walked up to me and shook my hand. It

turned out that Gage Gibby had two sons on my team and he'd been a ballplayer himself.

I could tell that he was a bright and happy guy who'd be a welcome addition to our team, and it turned out that he became exactly that.

Gage and I spent a week or two showing the kids the ropes and enjoying one day more than the one before.

We sat in small groups and talked about baseball—what they had seen, what they wanted to learn, what positions they wanted to play, what goals they had.

Some were shy at first, but they soon realized that we were all fishing from the same pond. Those talks were fantastic to the point where I really wish they'd been tape-recorded so I could listen to them again today.

One young boy, Johnny Stone, had been playing since he was eight. He really didn't like baseball and told me that more than once.

He'd been playing on Little League baseball teams for three seasons and had never even gotten ONE HIT in all that time.

His mom was quite ill and his dad often worked sixty or seventy hours a week. So they put him into sports programs against his wishes, and he always felt out of place on his teams.

The way he coped was by acting out. He'd make himself the goat in all of his antics. I figured that he was trying to mask his supposed lack of athletic ability by drawing attention to himself for anything other than sports.

Johnny missed a practice one night and I called his house to find out if there was anything wrong. He told me that he couldn't get a ride and wouldn't be able to come the next night either, for the same reason. I told him that I would pick him up.

I purposely got there about a half hour early and he was already sitting on his porch waiting for me. And since we had a little extra time, instead of going right to the ball field, we stopped at a local ice cream parlor and I bought him a cone.

We sat and talked about life and school and his parents and all kinds of things. And I could sense a trust forming.

All of his issues weren't going to be resolved in that short amount of time, but my goal as soon as I'd met him, was to assure him that he was just as important to our team as any other kid.

As we drove to the park, I told him, "*Remember when you told me that you've never even gotten one hit? Well, Johnny, this season you are going to get a hit, and it isn't going to be a little dribbler out in front of home plate or a fluke or anything like that.*"

"It's going to be a hard line drive into the outfield and you're going to get a double or a triple, and it's going to be a big hit too. And you are going to be so excited when you do it."

I told him to think about getting that first big hit whenever he had a bat in his hands because it could come at any time—and it will.

See the ball, hit the ball!

It actually shut him up for a few minutes. I knew he was going to do it. And I couldn't wait to see the look on his face when he finally smacked his first-ever base hit!

At our next practice, Johnny Stone showed up with his own pair of batting gloves!

There are lots of little boys with big dreams who are more than happy to tell you that they're gonna be in the big leagues someday.

These are happy and smart little kids. Most little boys are smart and happy and optimistic too.

Abraham Lincoln, "*Most people in this world are about as happy as they make up their minds to be."*

How about little Pete whose story I heard on television a while back regarding his experience with youth baseball. This fits like a glove with the concepts and ideas that I share in these writings.

Here's how little Pete's story unfolded:

"As a young boy, growing up, Pete loved playing baseball. That was his passion. But when he tried out for the team, the coach didn't even give him a chance. He said, "I'm sorry son, you're just too small. You will never be able to play on this team."

Pete was devastated His heart was set on playing baseball. His mom picked him up from school, and he and his best friend climbed into the backseat of the car. Pete was doing all he could to keep his composure, trying not to cry, and then his friend, who was much bigger than Pete, said, "Hey did you tell your mom you didn't make the team because you are too little?"

The friend's words pierced Pete's heart. He hated being small. He went home feeling low and dejected. Later that week though, the school made a special announcement, "Since so many boys tried out for the team, we are going to create a second team, a B team." Pete tried out for the B team and he made it.

That season, those two teams ended up in a playoff for the championship, and the B team beat the A team. Guess who the winning pitcher was? That's right, the B team won the championship, thanks to Pete's great pitching ability.

Now consider this question: How much potential did Pete have when he was rejected for the A team? Was his potential any different when he began pitching for the B team?

Bottom line: Other people's opinions do not determine your potential."

Unfortunately, Ace doesn't just determine your potential, he completely squashes it before you ever get any chance to give it a shot.

"Do unto others... "

You can view blatant examples of potential being squashed at any Little League field in Woonsocket and Jersey City and Marco Island and Salem and Albany...

Do you know what they call the guy who finishes last in medical school?

They call him Doctor!

He may have finished at the bottom of his class, but he did go through eight years of schooling earning him the right to treat, and heal, his patients.

Conversely, Little League coaches don't have five minutes of education. No exams, no certifications. They sign up and become the boss right away. Easy as pie.

It's as if they somehow earned Sergeant stripes on their first day! They friggin' love it! And you haven't lived until you hear Ace proudly introduce himself as the Head Coach!

They are so cute at that age...

Ace and many of his brethren are rarely in charge of anything anywhere else in their lives, so they take extreme delight in having the chance to puff out their chests at the Little League diamonds.

It's not difficult to spot these little straw bosses in San Jose and Nuremberg and Arlington and Rapid City and Milford...

Here's something that happens every night in Little League games across the world. Every single night.

Nearly every Little League coach will have his precious Ace Junior playing in the first inning of every game of the season.

Every game.

And Ace has players on his team who never get to play in the first inning of any game.

Any game.

Ace will deploy Ace Junior at a fixed defensive position, primarily at shortstop or second base, and if Junior is not playing at his usual defensive spot in a particular game, it's only because he's on the pitcher's mound that night.

And Ace has lots of games where he elects to have three different players rotating into, and out of, the game playing only two innings each in right field.

Let's do the math:

Ace Junior plays every one of the six innings in the ballgame. Then Ace has it cleverly set up so that three of Junior's teammates will only get to play two innings each in the same game.

As dumb as that sounds, it's further frightening to realize that Ace absolutely believes that he has cleverly unveiled a magnificent scheme that will catapult his team into the winner's circle.

But Ace really hasn't created one darn thing. These guys generally don't tend to score very high marks in creativity.

You see, there are hundreds of thousands of other coaching imbeciles who have employed the same foolish and harmful strategies while trying to win those cheap little trophies.

Most of you already clearly understand that these atrocious behaviors exist, but these Aces are so set in their ways that sometimes it takes them a little extra time to grasp these unmistakable truths!

But these malicious tactics will be in clear view again tonight in Muscatine and Ashland and Medway and St. Johnsbury and Las

Cruces...

For now.

This is my 59th year in baseball!

I've enjoyed more baseball perhaps than anybody who's ever lived. It has truly been the straw that has stirred my life's drink.

And I'm using every bit of my love for the game to educate and encourage anybody who's ever been associated with Little League Baseball.

We need to rid ourselves of the ugly prevailing sentiment which says, *"We've always done it this way."*

There was a time when there wasn't any way possible for me to speak individually with every Little League coach in every place that baseball is being played on this earth.

But with the advent of the Internet, it's now feasible for me to reach hundreds of thousands of these coaches at once! And that's extremely exciting for me.

And once you finish reading *Little Snowman Baseball*, you'll be certain that it takes just a minor adjustment to completely change the flavor of the Little League experience in Downers Grove and Ottawa and Broken Bow and Hastings and Upper Marlboro...

"If you think you 're too small to make a difference, try sleeping with a mosquito... "

Did you ever have the chance to visit Ace at his home?

He might begin by telling you about his Little League team and how they made it to the championship game. Or maybe he'll usher you into a room full of Little League trophies.

And you wouldn't need to be Einstein to realize that this guy has trampled the hopes and dreams of little kids—on his very own team!—in order to continue his quest for personal successes and the glory that comes along with reaching the Little League coaching mountaintop.

You'll be able to find Ace basking in more *glory* in Grand Forks and Waterbury and Auckland and Farmington and Ithaca...

Have you ever disciplined a child for doing something wrong by making certain that you selected the right words to ensure that he would never do it again?

I once had a life-changing conversation with a grown man who listened intently to every word I said. And he accepted my words in the spirit in which they were intended.

My friend Jerry was a power-lifter, a tri-athlete, a Yankee fan and a prankster. He was an awful lot of fun to be around.

Our Red Sox-Yankee debates were legendary. We always drew a crowd as people stopped to hear what we were hollering about!

One morning, Jerry mentioned that he had just begun his third season as a Little League coach. So we started having discussions about it. It coincided with the one year that I coached Little League myself.

It seemed as if every time he'd stop in, it would be to tell me about all the wonderful plays his son had been making. But I really never heard him talking about any of the other players on his team.

Sometimes Jerry would ask me a question about strategy or tell me about a play that happened the night before. But he really wasn't saying much other than highlighting his son's extraordinary exploits and then crowing about his own glowing won-loss record in the coaching ranks.

One morning, I asked Jerry if he had any players on his team that sat on the bench while his own remarkable son was on the field doing such amazing things.

"Of course I do", he responded. "I've got four kids that I play for one inning each, and I try to hide them in right field and left field. It works out perfectly."

I asked him quietly and simply,

"You do what?!! You hide kids?!! Are you crazy? Why on earth would you think to do something like that?"

I went on to gently read him the riot act—by telling him about Eddie Gaedel and Shaquille O'Neal and Michael Jordan— and then asked him if he had any idea what type of damage he might be doing to those kids who are just sitting and watching.

If he put a kid in right field for one inning a week, how much development would that youngster be experiencing?

Jerry's life changed forever in that little moment of enlightenment. His eyes were piercing mine as he listened, and I can't remember a time when a man paid more attention to me.

Tears were streaming down his face when he told me that he was going to change his ways the very next night at practice. He said that he felt ashamed and stupid for how he had been behaving.

If you've ever heard the expression *puppy dog eyes,* you would have seen *Exhibit A on Jerry's face.* This great big man was being humbled in a way that he'd never even contemplated.

The entire conversation lasted less than two minutes.

My simple thoughts made perfect sense to him. All I had done was ask a couple questions for which he had no answers, no rebuttals, no comebacks.

They were simply seed-planting questions that helped him to consider thinking about coaching Little League from a couple different angles other than his own—the little benchwarmer's viewpoint, as well as the perspective of the benchwarmer's parents.

He realized that he surely wouldn't want his own son to be treated like he was treating other people's kids.

It's important to realize that Jerry hadn't done anything wrong. He was doing what he thought was the right thing to do. He felt that he was supposed to be an evaluator of talent, and then go out and try to win the Little League title.

He'd seen Little League being coached that way his whole life and he was bound and determined to win championships, coach All-Star teams and be absolutely brilliant in the process.

There's no other way to slice it, Jerry was behaving the same way that Ace behaves.

In fact, JERRY WAS ACE!

And once he realized what he had been doing, he was ashamed of himself. Completely ashamed.

Jerry changed immediately—and radically. He told me that his whole team began enjoying the experience much more than ever before.

He didn't ease into his changes either. He modified his behavior right away, as he morphed into a totally different character altogether.

He was so proud of himself when he told me that his incredible son played just one inning in their game the night before. His pride and joy didn't even get into the game until the last inning either. He played right field and batted last in the batting order!

Jerry stopped by frequently to keep me posted on his progress. He told me that he finally realized that every player on the team wanted to learn how to play, and then have their chance to get on the field and show what they could do.

He told me that he still wanted to win, but his new thought

LITTLE SNOWMAN BASEBALL | Jake Snow

process made him understand that it just wasn't right to try and do so at all costs!

Jerry was the perfect example of the tiny tweaks of which I speak. One night is all it took!

All Jerry did was sit his little Ace Junior down on the pine for a while, and his life changed in the blink of an eye!

Do you know who else's life changed? Every one of those little benchwarmers—the ones Jerry had been completely ignoring—now had his full attention!

It's wonderful stuff that we are doing!

I've watched with joyful fascination when we have introduced *Little Snowman Baseball* in Campden and Lock Haven and Alpharetta and Tijuana and Green River...

Everything is beautiful in its own way.

Look! He's got the whole place to himself!

This kid has it made! He can stretch out as far as he wants. There's more than enough room. Heck, he could lay down and take a nap if he chose.

What the heck is he supposed to be thinking while he is sitting in there all by himself?

41

The biggest part of this problem is that Ace can look at one or two kids on his roster at the very first practice and dismiss them immediately.

Ace simply slots these little guys in as benchwarmers, many times upon first sight, and somehow feels totally justified in doing so!

And when Ace makes these types of befuddling decisions, it clearly indicates that he has decided to exercise his absolute power to immediately extinguish any chance those little guys might have had to play baseball.

Here's the way he thinks,

"Look at this kid, he can't even catch the ball. It looks like he's never even played before. I've got to figure out a way to play him as little as I can so that he doesn't cause us to lose any ballgames. He is terrible."

The scary part is that almost every kid who joins Little League is just beginning his baseball journey.

MANY OF THEM HAVE NEVER PLAYED BASEBALL BEFORE!

I suppose it never dawned on Ace to actually coach the kid so that he can get better. Instead, he has the sole focus of winning games. To him, the kids that he had turned into benchwarmers were nothing more than a thorn in his paw.

And to those kids who look up to him, with hope in their hearts, and wanting to play so badly, Ace looks like a giant standing in their way.

Does playing the role of giant make any sense of any kind? I ask you Ace, and I want you to really think about this,

"Do you still feel small when you stand beside the ocean?"

My kids played all over the field on defense.

Every kid on our roster had a chance to play every position that he wanted to play during the season.

When I sent them out on the field to play defense each inning, they would all hover around me holding their gloves, and they'd be ready to sprint in whichever direction I sent them.

Our defensive positions changed every inning of the season.

One time, after most of my defense was set, I realized that I hadn't sent anybody out to right field yet. I looked at Coach Gibby's son and told him that he could go play out there.

And it surprised the heck out of me when he told me that "*Right field is for losers!*" I couldn't believe that he said that.

I wondered what Hank Aaron and Reggie Jackson and Babe Ruth might have thought if they heard him say that "Right field is for losers"! Some of the greatest stars in the history of baseball played in right field!

So I said to him,, "*OK, tell you what big boy, right now you are a bench fielder. Have a seat right here next to me.*"

When his dad came in from warming up the pitcher, I told him what had just happened.

Gage whirled around and asked his son, "*Did Coach Snow tell you to play right field?*" The kid nodded sheepishly.

43

Coach Gibby finished his thoughts by saying, *"If Coach tells you to play right field, you play right field. If he tells you to play third base, you play third base. If he tells you to play Checkers, you play Checkers!"*

Cracked me up.

How'd the kid take it? Well, at the little banquet that we had after the season, he came up to me as the team representative and handed me a present. He wanted me to open it.

And...

It was a box of Checkers!

Three years later, he was the starting RIGHT FIELDER for the High School Varsity baseball team.

And he was a darn good one too!

I was warming up behind the dugout before our Little League game with the Cardinals.

I had won my first four games as the starting pitcher for the Cubs and began to believe that my pitches were unhittable. And I was a nine-year-old kid thinking like that!

I've always had supreme confidence playing sports, especially baseball.

My inner dialogue sounded like this, *"These poor kids won't even have a chance today What's the record for strikeouts in this joint?!!"*

As those ideas and others were bouncing around in my head, suddenly I heard nearby voices having a conversation about the teams in the league.

I wasn't able to see the two kids who were talking, but I could hear them as clear as a bell. They were sitting on the dugout bench, but it was made of wood, instead of chain link, so my vision was blocked out.

They were going back and forth talking about the different pitchers they'd batted against so far.

More than a little bit interested, my ears really perked up when they began talking about me!

One kid said, "*You know, it's really funny to watch Jake Snow when he pitches. He has that great big windup, and then he throws his left leg way up in the air like Juan Marichal does for the San Francisco Giants, and then this really, really slow ball comes floating out of his hand...*"

He might have said more, but it didn't register with me if he had. My spirits were crushed. His words had devastated me. I thought I had the best fastball in the whole league and these kids were talking as if I were throwing little bloopers up to home plate.

A jury of my peers had essentially rearranged the entire landscape of my mind.

Too young to understand psychology then—and, still to this day, I don't know if those kids said those things for my benefit—my emotions ran the gamut from "*Boy I didn't realize that I looked like a freak on the mound*" to "*Now I will never pitch in the World Series!*"

A little guy who had dreamed night and day about becoming a big leaguer was now forced to make other plans. The mind can be quite complicated.

My normal focus was always on the catcher's mitt. But that night, I was dealing with the lingering effects of those pre-game comments.

The first batter struck out and so did the second one. Their third hitter popped one up to our shortstop. In the second inning, I struck out all three batters!

How were these guys missing my REALLY slow pitches?

Meanwhile, we took the lead by eight or nine runs, and the game appeared to be going our way, when the top of the third inning rolled around.

Then I had an idea. I made up my mind to actually throw a ball as softly as I could. If they wanted to see me throw a slow one, then I was going to accommodate them.

With two outs in the third, I had already retired the first eight batters so I figured that it was as good a time as any to test out my theory.

The hitter dug in and I flipped the ball toward the plate as soft as soft could be. And that little bugger RIPPED that baseball harder than any kid had ever hit one off me before. It was smoked!

And, as if it had eyes, the baseball was flying straight towards me. Before I could react, and get my glove up, the ball hit me squarely in my chest and knocked me right onto the ground! I didn't pass out, but I was fearful that I might.

Every Little Leaguer's nightmare came true when my mother sprinted from the grandstand to the mound to tend to her little boy. And it seemed like everybody who attended that game was standing around me in a circle.

A minute later, I was back on my feet and all my moving parts were working just fine. But, from that day to this, whenever I'm playing a sport, I play the game as hard as I can and nobody can talk me out of it!

I learned that lesson and I learned it well.

When I was a little kid, everybody called me Jakey—little Jakey Snow.

My mom called me Jakey until the day she went to heaven. All five of my sisters still call me Jakey. My dad sometimes called me Admiral because of my Navy days.

But as I got older, most people simply shortened my name to Jake—without even asking me. I guess it's the way of the world.

But little JAKEY never went anywhere. Jakey never grew up. Baseball was my first love and it will be my last. Life is a bowl of cherries when you know what you want and I was smitten with the world's greatest game on the first day that I discovered it.

I can still remember exactly how innocently it started too. Dad came outside after supper and told me to come back into the house. He said, *"Jakey, come inside. I want you to hear something. You'll like this."*

He tuned the radio to the Red Sox game and told me to listen. He may not have had any idea what he had just done, but it cemented a lifetime of happiness for me.

I was only four years old.

While listening to that game, the announcer kept talking about a player named Carl Yastrzemski. Yaz—that's what they nicknamed him—was a young star outfielder for the Boston Red Sox. What a cool name!

His name, more than likely, was the primary reason that he immediately became my favorite player. And I made a very good choice too because he went on to play for 24 seasons in his very special Hall of Fame baseball career.

Dad told people many times that I could spell *Yastrzemski* before I could even spell *Snow*!

Whether that was a fact, or merely a bit of tongue-in-cheek fiction, baseball was the sole reason that I was motivated to learn how to read even before I went to Kindergarten.

Every summer morning, as a five-year-old, I'd sit on my front porch at 5 AM waiting for the kid to bring the newspaper. He really didn't have to bring it because I already knew everything I needed to know. I just wanted to see it in black and white.

47

We didn't have around the clock coverage on cable, satellites, or the Internet in those days. In fact, Red Sox games were only televised on Friday nights and Sunday afternoons.

The rest of the action had to be listened to on the radio. Oh and was it ever!! Every day, every pitch, every season, ever since!

Oddly, the way that I coached was viewed as unorthodox.

I did the unthinkable. I let every one of my little guys play lots of baseball at every game. Every kid got to hit leadoff, and bat cleanup, and in every other spot in the batting order too.

All of them also had the opportunity to sit on the bench for multiple innings in every game too.

Stop the presses!

Who in their right mind would operate in such a manner?!

One opposing coach felt the need to tell me that I didn't know what the heck I was doing because I had my best player batting last in our lineup.

But since the players on my team batted in the order that they arrived at the field, his observation made perfect sense to me.

I guess I confused a number of people.

But these crazy methods of mine work beautifully in Point Pleasant and Laredo and Quebec and Pahrump and Saginaw...

Years ago, I founded a talent agency.

I learned a lot about people during that time.

A former shipmate—Marty—and I opened a photography studio soon after he finished his studies at a Liberal Arts college in Kansas City.

I owned a big commercial building and there were two vacant

LITTLE SNOWMAN BASEBALL | Jake Snow

offices across from our second-floor studio.

Two enterprising women rented that space to produce dance recitals for young girls and boys. And their business caught fire and took off like a moon rocket.

They needed lots of modeling photographs to be taken, so we wound up joining forces with them, and the cash came pouring in almost as if we were printing money!

Marty asked what my thoughts were on possibly representing some of the youngsters professionally. It was an excellent question because a number of them sure seemed to possess star qualities.

I could easily see how talented many of these young kids were—singing, dancing, playing instruments—and I remembered that my own media agent, Peter Jordan, was already in business in New York City.

I called Peter to ask for his advice on how I might get some exposure for these young *future starlets*.

Crazy enough, on that very call, I learned that Peter and his partner had just created an additional revenue stream for themselves by representing up-and-coming entertainers.

The timing was incredible.

Peter told me that my new company was going to be the first talent agency in his stable. Grin. I'd just hung out our shingle three days earlier!

Suddenly our photo studio shifted from primarily shooting weddings and portraits to making beautiful headshots for aspiring young models and actors!

And our business exploded too. It was remarkable how fast we grew and how much revenue we were generating. It was like we had just opened our own casino!

Here's an example of what began happening throughout the

entire city:

Your neighbor stops over to tell you about how she had just signed up her daughter at a local talent agency. And she added that her youngster had professional photos taken that would help her be discovered by talent scouts down in New York City.

Bubbling over with excitement, the woman tells you how her daughter was gonna have a chance to be in magazines and catalogs and TV commercials, and maybe even a movie down the line! The woman was fired up!

When she leaves, you turn to your spouse right away and say, *"Our kid is so much better looking than her kid. We should sign Molly up for this too. Molly has a way better chance of being discovered than our neighbor's kid!"*

And, sure enough, on the following Saturday, Molly and her parents are right there in my crowded reception area where the next round of budding young superstars were assembled.

These people would give you any amount of money that you asked them to give you. And that's because they knew, in their hearts, that it would be their kids who would be the ones destined for fame and fortune.

There was no end in sight either! And the exact same thing is going on in your home town right this minute, and I don't even know where you live!

The reason for that is because we all feel that our kids are the coolest, smartest, best-looking, and brightest of them all. And that is why the world works!

Some of my little aspiring actresses did wind up getting a gig here or there, but most of them didn't even get a sniff of stardom. I remember taking our Head Shot books down to New York and sitting with the talent scouts. They'd whiz through those books as if they were shuffling cards.

Every Snow Often, they'd stop and point at a photo and tell me to have the kid come down to New York for a catalog shoot or a local commercial or whatever else they might have been seeking at that particular time.

It wasn't long though before I decided to lend my focus to other business pursuits. Being a talent scout just wasn't for me. I felt like I was hurting more people than I was helping.

Heck, even the ones who were fortunate enough to get some work might not have even finished in the black.

The kid might earn $800 for a catalog photo shoot, but the family would incur the expense of traveling to New York, missing a day or two from work, staying overnight in a hotel, and it just didn't seem to make very much sense to me.

We will all do anything we can for our kids and this same mindset definitely spills over onto the Little League fields.

And all Ace needs to realize is that Junior is not necessarily cooler than all of the other kids.

Most of us didn't have dreams of coaching when we were little kids.

Instead we planned on launching long home runs or striking out a big slugger to end the World Series! Those dreams stayed alive inside us for as long as we played. But one day that flame flickered and went out for the final time—and our playing days were over.

I was luckier than most of us dreamers because I played my last hardball game when I was 52 years old.

But just because 99% of us didn't make it to the big leagues, it doesn't mean that we didn't try!

And the story doesn't have to end there because when you have kids of your own, those dreams begin anew, don't they? It could be that it's Ace Junior who is destined to play under the bright lights instead of you!

So it would make perfect sense that Ace would take the Head Coaching position and coach him all the way to the big leagues!

Or maybe until he is twelve-years-old.

Would someone be able to coach in Little League if he didn't know very much about baseball?

He may have very little knowledge simply because he didn't get a chance to play baseball while growing up. Or perhaps, sports were just never a big part of the landscape in their homes.

And if that's the case, you might figure that you'd be at a huge disadvantage against coaches who've been around baseball for many years.

Not necessarily.

First things first, you'd no doubt wind up being a much better coach than Ace simply by applying the common sense God gave you.

"The thing about common sense is that it's not that common." – Voltaire

Coaching Little Leaguers isn't a job that requires tremendous amounts of information known only to a select few. It's baseball. That's all there is to it.

No matter what league, city, state, or country—three strikes and three outs is all you really need to know.

My advice for fathers and mothers, who believe they'd like to try their hand at coaching, is to do a little bit of pre-emptive work beforehand.

Don't wait until the first practice is coming up the following week. Begin thinking about what kind of coach you'd like to be. Read about baseball. Watch baseball. Play baseball.

Look online and find—and then learn—some of the fun drills you can do at your practices. Go to a baseball camp if you can. See if it is really something you want to do.

If it turns out that it's fun and interesting for you, that means you can make it fun and interesting for the kids too.

And if you happen to really enjoy yourself, maybe down the line you can coach some high school ball or local amateur teams.

Bottom line: The lessons you teach at the Little League level are the same lessons on display in the big leagues!

The game doesn't change.

Although in 1859, the home plate umpire called balls and strikes while sitting in a rocking chair, but that's neither here nor there!

In the dead of Winter, my son and I stopped at Clayton Park— the baseball field where he was going to be playing his games that Spring.

Benjamin had never played baseball on a diamond with bases that were ninety feet apart before. In Little League, there's only sixty feet between the bases.

The field was covered with mounds of snow and sheets of ice, so all we could see was about one third of the outfield fence.

One of the *Townies* told me that a kid named Barry O'Donnell smashed a home run over that left field fence in 1965, and nobody had cleared it ever since.

Silently, I wondered if my little buddy might be the next kid to whack one over that wall.

About a week later, I was contacted by the Minnesota Twins who had a proposition for me.

Of all the different types of sports broadcasting I had done, I had never been a play-by-play announcer for a professional baseball team. And that had always been one of my strongest desires.

I found a job board for on-air talent and offered teams an open invitation stating that I would be available on short notice—even for short term assignments—because I was highly motivated to do it.

That's how the Twins found me. Their announcer was on medical leave and wasn't scheduled to return until May. We signed a six week contract with a renewal clause in case it were to last a bit longer.

It was Double-A baseball in Florida and it gave me the opportunity to escape the final nasty month of another cruel New England winter.

It also meant that I'd be missing ten or twelve of Benjamin's games at the beginning of his season. My daughter had a dance recital and a play scheduled during that time too.

To make up for it, I made them a deal. When school got out in May, they would fly to Florida and we would go to Disney and Sea World and Wet 'n Wild and Epcot and all the rest.

On the day that I was leaving, it was so cold outside that when I tried to close the door of my Jeep, the latch had frozen and it wouldn't close! BRRR!!!

It was a perfect day to escape New England en route to the sunshine of Florida where I would be meeting the fresh young faces of the St. Augustine Friars!

The Friars played a game in Lakeland on a Saturday afternoon in April. In the top of the third inning, the skies opened up and everybody ran for cover. Forecasts were for a rain delay of an hour or more.

While we were waiting for the storm to subside, Benjamin's mom called on my cell and, when I picked up the call, she was already in full throat, *"You missed it, Daddy, you missed it!"*

Smiling I said, *"What, pray tell, did I miss?"*

She laughed and said, *"Jake, Benjamin just smashed one all the way out here to left field and it hit right at the top of the fence! It was amazing. And somebody told me that nobody has hit it over that fence in more than FORTY years!"*

She was so excited and it was wonderful to listen to her bubbling over with such enthusiasm.

When there was a break in her story, I piped up, *"Thanks for calling me. I appreciate it. I really do. But don't tell Benjamin that you called me. I don't want him to say, I know Mom told you already. I want him to tell me the story from the top."*

She laughed, understood, and agreed.

Benjamin's call came in about fifteen minutes after our game went final. It was funny because he began telling me about the ballgame itself, but I already knew the exciting conclusion so it was neat listening to how he was picking and choosing his words as he went along.

He normally didn't talk nearly as much as his sister and I do. We are chatterboxes, so we spend most of our time on Transmit.

Benjamin primarily spent his time on Receive.

He'd hear everything and soak it up like a sponge. He was never just waiting for the other person to stop talking so he could chime right in to the conversation!

"Don't listen so you can respond. Listen so you can understand."

I could tell that he was ramping up a bit and it didn't take long before he got to his happy ending,

"And Dad, in the sixth inning, I hit one way over the left fielder's head. You know how I always have trouble keeping my helmet on

my head when I have to run fast, so I was trying to hold it with my right hand when I was racing toward first, and then I looked out to where the ball was and saw it hit right near the top of the fence!"

"Dad, it was the best shot ever! He didn't field the ball cleanly either, so when he went to pick it up, I rounded second base and got an easy triple. It was probably a double and an error, Dad. Whaddya think?"

I answered excitedly,

"I think I wish I were in Maine earlier today! God love ya, son! Good job! And if you hit the ball that far, I think that a triple would be the appropriate scoring on the play ."

The Friars had Monday night off so I decided to go visit one of the Radiomen from my old ship. Frankie Waska and I were swapping tall tales on his back porch when Benjamin called about eight thirty.

And, right out of the chute, a very excited voice came booming through the phone,

"Dad! Dad! Not only did I hit it over the fence in left field tonight, but it went over the road and HALFWAY UP THE TREES! Dad, I did it, I killed it!"

I chuckled as I briefly thought about how his first coach had decided that Benjamin wasn't even good enough to play Little League baseball.

Ace never let him start a game that year. He batted him last in every lineup and the only position he ever let Benjamin play was out in right field.

Now Benjamin was crushing baseballs into places where baseballs hadn't gone in nearly a half-century!

And wrongs are now being made right in Fairfax and Tacoma and Deadwood and Ogunquit and Kokomo...

Just to be clear, Ace...

I don't really care if the Founding Fathers of your fair city thought so much of your baseball knowledge and skills that they've erected statues of you at every point of egress in and out of the city limits.

The Town Elders were undoubtedly unaware that part of your coaching blueprint was to abuse your Little League coach's *absolute power,* and use it to turn normal every day kids into benchwarmers.

One benchwarmer is one too many.

And it's *one too many* in Dorchester and Morehead City and Paducah and Savannah and Overland Park...

You'll get a kick out of this

At the end of each season, Little League coaches cast votes for the All Star team representatives from their teams.

This is primitive. Every league is different in how they operate. I'm simply illustrating a point, as is my custom.

For the sake of simplicity, let's say that there are ten teams in the league and each coach gets to select one player from their team.

And since each coach has a mindset that Ace Junior is the best player on the team, or at least the second best, Ace will inevitably choose his own little prodigy as the team's lone All-Star representative.

Do you know how I chose my All-Star representatives for our team during the season that I coached?

I did it blindfolded. I put all their names into a batting helmet and chose my All-Stars that way. To me, they were all All-Stars!

"There's such balance in nature."

But follow the bouncing ball here:

Let's say that each one of the coaches have spent the whole season watching their Ace Junior playing shortstop—the most important defensive position.

For the sake of argument, this means that it's possible for all ten of the league's All-Stars to have played shortstop all year long.

And because every single one of them were installed at shortstop at the very first practice of the year, it follows that none of them would have played defensively at any other position all season, unless you count the time they spent on the pitcher's mound.

Obviously, only one of those little Ace Juniors is going to be able to play shortstop on the All-Star team, right? They can't all stand in the same spot!

That means that the other nine kids would have to go find a new position to play! Crazy huh?!

One of them would even have to go out and play right field which is supposedly the wasteland where benchwarmers go to play for their one or two innings per game.

One of these little heirs to the throne is gonna have to suck it up and be the right fielder.

And Ace Junior will mope the entire time he's out there too. He figures that playing right field is far beneath him. Ace has repeatedly driven that point home.

Junior firmly believes that he is a shortstop. He's played shortstop ever since he started playing in Little League. And not so amazingly, Junior playing shortstop coincided exactly with the moment when Ace began coaching him!

So the head coach of the All-Star team fills out the rest of the defense with his band of merry shortstops, but then he ran out of spots on the field, right?!

58

Ten kids. And only nine positions to play on defense. Uh-Oh, Spaghetti-O!

One of the Ace Juniors has to sit on the BENCH! There's no other place for him to play!

That tenth Ace Junior, another *supposedly talented shortstop*, has to sit on the bench and watch the action unfold the same way that his benchwarmer teammates had to do all season.

And Junior isn't gonna like sitting there, not even a little bit.

It would give me great pleasure to study Ace's facial gestures because he'll most certainly display exactly how mortified he is in this time of great turmoil for him.

And we know that during the regular season, Ace didn't pay one ounce of attention to the kids that he himself had turned into benchwarmers.

Karma is a beautiful thing.

Imagine if you're a guy who coaches the same way that Ace does, and that fact is becoming increasingly more evident to you every time you turn a page.

And if you have been acting the same way that Ace behaves, it's probably sinking in by now that you're not going to be able to get away with your dreadful behavior any longer.

It wouldn't surprise me one bit if you were to get down into the fetal position in order to protect yourself. You feel anger, nervousness, and agitation because you believed that you were operating under the radar.

"Don't pay any attention to that man behind the curtain."

Maybe you are furious with me for having the audacity to shine a light into your dark and secret places. People under stress frequently seek to shoot the messenger.

My words may sound as if I'm constantly lashing out at Ace, but that's not necessarily the case.

It would only take two seconds for Ace to flip the script. How?

All Ace would have to do is to simply leave Ace Junior out of the starting lineup at the next game.

That's all Ace needs to do.

And once he can summon the strength and awareness to put Junior on the bench for the start of a game, then he is no longer an Ace!

The problem is that Ace simply can't find it within himself to do something like that to Ace Junior.

So we need to find a way to convince him.

And I know that Ace is currently being convinced in Des Plaines and Morgan City and Telluride and Douglasville and Meridian...

My coaching style seemed to come as a surprise to many people.

And there were reasons for that! I confused a lot of folks with the style I created—and then adopted.

My entire life had been dedicated to baseball and I knew it was a game for everybody, not just for a select few.

Unorthodox? How's this?

Our batting order was different for every game. I certainly was not up nights pacing the floor agonizing over which Little Leaguer should bat before or after another one!

In fact, I did not construct the batting order at all. I let the kids make out the lineup card themselves.

Huh?

The kids who got to the field first would be the first ones to hit in the batting order. If they were the first one to get there, they'd be the leadoff batter that night.

Here's how I did it:

I would drive to the field at around 2:30 and tape a lineup card on the dugout fence. The game wouldn't start until six, but some of those little buggers would get on their bikes right after school and have their names on that card by 3:15! They LOVED it.

The other coaches figured that we would probably finish in last place after they had pillaged my roster at the Preseason Draft. In their views, they had left me with the runt of the litter.

But guess what happens when half of the little ballplayers on your team show up three hours before game time?

Some days, when I had a little extra time available, I'd come back to the field and we'd have a little batting practice or else we'd work on some of our fundamental fielding and running drills.

Guess what? They started to get better, a whole lot better!

Every kid had filled out a card telling me all the positions they wanted to play that season. And they were guaranteed to play every position that they had written down.

The only exception was for the ones who wanted to pitch. If a kid couldn't reach the plate in the air, he wasn't going to be able to throw strikes. So I didn't put him on the mound until he was able to do that, thus saving him from any embarrassment.

But all they had to do was keep practicing and as soon as they could throw it over the plate consistently, they'd be on that mound the next night.

This way, they could "*Fire when Ready!*"

Every one of them got the chance to bat leadoff and be our cleanup hitter too. It was music to their ears when they got to hear their names called with the chance to bat in those special places in the lineup!

By using the re-entry rule, where a player can be replaced in the lineup and then return later on in the game, the amount of baseball that each kid played became simple mathematics.

If I had a dozen players that night, only nine could be in the field at once. So the formula was easy to figure out.

Nine kids would be stationed around the diamond for each of the six innings in the game. That added up to fifty-four potential positions to play on defense.

Then I divided fifty-four by my twelve players, and learned that every kid would play at least four innings, and six of them would have the chance to play five innings.

Yes, everybody got to play a lot of baseball every night. And every one of them spent their share of the time on the bench time too.

They were all treated the same.

These unusual coaching behaviors might ring as nutty and foolish to the *old guard*, but these kids were nine, ten and eleven years old.

A trust developed between our players and coaches. They knew they would be treated fairly and they also knew we had expectations of them too.

Two or three times that season, I handed out a baseball quiz for them to take home and bring back. This gave them a chance to talk about baseball with their moms and dads and brothers and sisters.

Everybody always did great on those fun little tests. And the ones who didn't do as well were able to find out the answers when we talked about them at the next practice or game.

Finally—it was time for us to play our first game.

They all had their uniforms on with their new hats. The field was freshly lined. It was time to play some ball!

I remember Benjamin coming up to bat for the first time in his life. He got drilled in the left leg on the first pitch he ever saw. In the process, he knocked in the first run of his life because the bases were loaded when he stepped into the batter's box.

And his first time up in his second season, he knocked in a run again. He knocked himself in! He smashed that baseball so high and deep to left field that it cleared the fence by forty feet!

I watched that ball soaring out of the ballpark and quickly looked back at him. He didn't even watch it! First, he tried to cram his huge helmet back on his head, and then he just started sprinting around the bases.

I was coaching first base and watched him run past me faster than I'd ever seen him run before. When he got to third base, Coach Gibby was telling him, "*Benjamin! Slow down! Enjoy it!*"

And I bet he was enjoying it plenty! Just a few short weeks earlier, Benjamin told us he didn't want to play baseball anymore because Ace had treated him so poorly the year before.

Ace had Benjamin firmly convinced that he didn't even belong on a Little League baseball team.

What a difference a year makes?

Have you ever played the game called Boggle?

It's a fast-paced word game where players race against one another while trying to find as many words as they can by chasing down patterns of letters found on sixteen little cubes.

You play against your opponents and you also play against the clock—an egg timer.

I always enjoyed playing *Boggle* and became quite good at it. My mind works exceptionally fast, and I love words, so it made sense that I would enjoy playing the game.

One day, I'd been showing my kids how to play and left the game out on the dining room table.

My friend, Dougie, stopped over that night and spotted the Boggle game. He asked me about it and told me that he would like to play it sometime.

A couple nights later, he showed up again, and we sat down to play Boggle. I explained it to him and we flipped over the timer and got right down to business. When the smoke cleared, I had beaten him 98-4.

Most people in his shoes would have said something like,

"WOW! You killed me! Holy Smokes! I could never beat you at this game. That was amazing!"

But not only did he not say that, he said,

"Let's do that again."

After that, Dougie came to my place week after week and never gave up. And he kept getting better, as the margin of my victories were decreasing all the time.

One night, he handed me a brand new fire-engine red Boston Red Sox baseball cap. It had a big **B** on it, and he wanted it to be forever known as the official Reigning *Boggler* crown.

And the reason for giving that to me was because he felt that he was getting ready to take me down in the very near future.

By his own estimates, Dougie believed I had beaten him more than a thousand games in a row! He also told me that he was going to hire a band to march past my house on the day after he beat me.

He may never know how proud I was of him because he kept playing so hard trying to get over that magical hump—the day when he would wear the *Reigning Boggier* crown for the very first time!

So many people are sore losers, and most of them would have never played again following that first lopsided loss. But Dougie pressed on. He had it in him to continue to battle his way toward something that he really wanted to accomplish.

He had an amazing inner spirit and drive, the kind only available to the strongest of men.

Then he finally did it! He raised his right fist in celebration. He did an exaggerated triple fist pump. He got on his feet and danced! This was a three-hundred-pound man loving life to its fullest.

Think Dancing Bear!

It was a moment that will be frozen forever in time. It was beautiful. I took the *Reigning Boggier* crown off my head and ceremoniously placed it on his big bald dome.

When he showed up to play the next night, he strode through that door wearing that *Reigning Boggler* crown with a visible sense of accomplishment and satisfaction.

Dougie had every reason to feel that way and I was appropriately happier for him than he was for himself.

I tell that story on these pages because there are little kids that watch the big leaguers on television and want to grow up and be just like them.

Obviously, if they were to go onto a major league diamond when they are only ten-years-old, the odds against them would be ridiculous and they'd have absolutely no chance.

But if they consistently practice and apply the new skills that they learn, by the time they reach the physical and mental stages where they could actually compete, they'd be ready to take on all comers!

Remember there was once a High School coach who also told fourteen-year-old Shaquille O'Neal that he was "*too big, too slow and too clumsy"* and cut him from the basketball team.

Another High School coach in North Carolina told Michael Jordan that he wasn't good enough to play on his basketball team either.

Let that marinate in your mind one more time!

And those idiotic decisions were made by coaches who were actually qualified—and paid—to make those kinds of decisions.

Willie Mays went oh-for-five at the plate in his first game in the big leagues and ended up going hitless in his first twelve at bats. Willie Mays went on to hit 660 home runs and is widely regarded as one of the greatest legends of the game.

Once again, do you believe that you should rob a young child of an opportunity to explore the desires of his heart? How do you know the size of the kid's heart? How do you know what's in that heart?

The short answer is that YOU DON'T!

You could have another Dougie in your midst, somebody who wouldn't quit until he got where he wanted to go.

And you can find a *Dougie* everywhere you look in Tempe and Youngstown and Stillwater and Great Falls and Rochester...

There's a little boy in your town who is up in his bedroom right now thinking about baseball.

He's tossing a ball up in the air a thousand times dreaming about becoming a big leaguer someday.

He watches every game that he can. He listens to them on the radio when it's his bedtime.

He's often outside throwing a ball against any surface where it will bounce back to him. He's the pitcher, the catcher, the shortstop, the batter, the runner—heck, he just wants to play.

He LOVES baseball and can't wait for the day when he can be on a team. He wants to learn and play and enjoy. He wants to imitate his favorite players.

He shows up at practice on that first day. He's been waiting for years. The big day has finally arrived! His mom had circled it on the refrigerator calendar and he's been counting down by marking X's every day until it was finally time to play some baseball.

But with a stroke of your pen, you instantly write him off because he apparently didn't pass muster from *your keen eye for talent*. You immediately pencil him in as a benchwarmer, right at the very first practice.

Boom! It's done. Your decision has been made. That kid's fate is sealed. One or two innings is the most he'll ever play in a game.

It doesn't matter that Ace Junior comes home from school every afternoon and plays video games on his phone for hours.

Ace Junior would much rather play with his electronic toys instead of playing baseball anyway. Often these kids aren't necessarily thrilled about playing baseball, but they don't want to upset or disappoint their parents.

Plus, Junior already knows that he'll be in the starting lineup every game anyway, simply because Ace is his coach. He doesn't need to do anything to sharpen his skills to play.

Ace Junior doesn't need to do anything at all.

That's because Junior knows people in high places. He already has the key to the Executive Washroom.

I wonder if he washes his hands.

Let's spend a moment together in Ace's brain,

"Ace Junior is going to pitch and play shortstop. He'll either bat

leadoff or cleanup in my batting order. Another guy's kid is going to play right field for one inning per game but that's only because they make me play all the kids on the team."

Don't kid yourself. Whether Ace does this consciously, or not, is beside the point. They ALL do it. And most of them take the coaching position with a burning desire to win a championship.

As you read along, my position is to make Ace begin to understand that he would actually have more fun than he'd ever had, if he would simply flip-flop that little benchwarmer with Ace Junior!

"Blasphemy! Ace Junior is so much better than that other kid."

And that's precisely the problem, Ace.

"Forgive them father for they know not what they do."

I'm pointing out what's been happening for more than seventy five years, and it's never gonna stop happening until everybody reads my words—or words similar to these—so together we can create this simple change that's so easy for us to implement.

"Do the best you can until you know better. Then when you know better, do better." – Maya Angelou

And now we are watching Ace do better in Ogden and Hastings and Trenton and Montgomery and Joplin…

There is something very beautiful in baseball that we don't think about nearly enough.

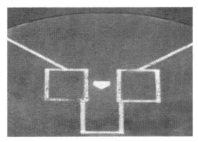

I'm talking about the recently manicured white chalk lines that run from home plate all the way to the outfield fences. I love how the batter's box looks when it is newly chalked!

When you see those white lines gleaming like that, you know that the game is ready to begin! They don't make those beautiful markings in the dirt until it's time to play some baseball!

What made me think of this right now is because I was remembering my first game ever, when I got a chance to bat leadoff that day.

And the batter's box was chalked just the way they are in the big leagues! What a rush it was for a nine-year-old to climb into that batter's box when everything was so shiny and tidy. I was so happy!

Imagine the kid who never gets to bat until the last inning. He doesn't get a chance to get into a batter's box before those chalk lines have all been completely rubbed away and gone forever. It's just a big pile of dirt by the time he gets his turn at the plate.

I bet Ace Junior gets to see those chalk lines up close and personal in the first inning of every game, doesn't he?

Did you ever think about that, Ace?

"I'm the greatest hitter in the world!"

The little boy throws the ball up in the air and then swings his bat and misses.

He tries to hit it a bunch of times, but he's just unable to make contact between the bat and ball.

But he doesn't gets discouraged one little bit.

The next thing he does is toss the ball up in the air again,

"I'm the greatest pitcher in the world!"

And it brings him great delight when he is still unable to hit it.

The kid loves baseball and wants to learn to play it. Then he gets his dose of Ace.

And then he can say , *"I'm the greatest benchwarmer in the world*!"

"I had a friend who was a big baseball player

Back in high school,

He could throw that speedball by you

Make you look like a fool.."

Those are the first couple lines of Bruce Springsteen's *Glory Days*. His friend never advanced forward one more inch, either in baseball or in life, once his high school heroics had ended.

So he spends a good deal of his time reliving the only part of his life where he did feel special.

At least it was high school!

Imagine a guy using his Little League coaching days as his own personal *Glory Days*?

Oh, believe me, there are plenty of coaches who fit this profile perfectly.

Way too many!

Don't kid yourself. Some of these guys actually shine their trophies every chance they get.

And there will be more *shining* again tonight in Harrisburg and Vancouver and Carson City and Plattsburgh and Madrid...

Take a quick glance at the one of the Little Snowman Baseball cover illustrations that a cartoonist made for me.

The littlest kid with the biggest bat taking the mightiest swing.

Who cares if he hits it?

As long as he gets to swing it!

And the great news is that Ace is finally letting him *swing it* as hard as he wants in Cedar Rapids and Spokane and Flagstaff and Newton and Sarasota...

I met a middle-aged woman last year, and she was sharing a few of her thoughts from yesteryear.

"My husband coached our kids when they were little and they all had so much fun."

"Our kids were good players too. I remember that we won the championship one time. It was great!"

She was no doubt telling me the God's honest truth through her prism. Many moms have memories like that. They love their kids, and they remember them as little kids playing baseball and having fun with their friends.

But she may not have had the same happy memories if it were her own son who sat on the bench, instead of getting the preferential treatment that her little Ace Junior received from his coaching father!

Think about Ace's wife sitting on the bleachers right next to another mother who is also there to support her kid. But the other mom's son always has to sit on the bench most of the night.

Believe it or don't, there are people sitting on those bleachers who look at the parents of the benchwarmers, and somehow feel superior to them for one reason or another.

Happens all the time. It's ridiculous.

But it happens every night in Flagstaff and Barstow and Fairbanks and Peabody and Jacksonville...

There has never been a moment when I didn't enjoy watching young kids play baseball.

Having had the chance to coach them made it all that much sweeter for me. Teaching them the game I've loved since I was a preschooler was awesome.

One of the easiest lessons to teach kids was that hustling was the best evidence that you were giving it everything you've got whenever you were on that field.

I'd tell my players that if they were trying their best, I didn't care if they missed the ball and it rolled a hundred feet past them.

It was no problem for me, even if they ran the wrong way on the bases, as long as they were hustling.

Actually, the best way to learn is by making mistakes!

Even if you swing and miss ten times in a row, that simply means that you are that much closer to smacking the next pitch to Timbuktu!

Mistakes are OK!!!

I've seen way too many little players, on far too many teams, being yelled and screamed at for throwing to the wrong base or booting a ground ball or dropping a popup.

Let them play. Let them grow. Let them learn!

"When you have someone who believes in you, that's when you can go as high as you want" – **Unknown**

How 'bout this?

I try not to leave any stone unturned on this subject. Give me a minute here to let something else enter your consciousness.

We've already established that every team has a kid, or more than one kid, who is considered a benchwarmer. He only gets to play the minimum amount of time as mandated by the league. This usually means one inning in the field and one time at bat.

And sometimes Ace will unbelievably send up a pinch hitter to bat for the kid when it's finally time for him to get to swing the bat!

That kid wants to play. He is so excited. Maybe it's his only chance to be like the other kids.

Maybe he has a stutter or he's nervous or shy or hungry or he could have sight or hearing problems yet to be diagnosed.

Maybe he's got internal injuries from being beaten at home. Sick parents? Broken Home? Heck, he could be homeless for all you know!

And you won't know either because you have more important fish to fry, like maneuvering your batting order and setting up those all-important defensive alignments.

Or maybe that kid is just as happy and healthy and well-adjusted as Ace Junior.

But for some reason, known only to you, the youngster just happened to wind up on the wrong side of your guillotine blade. He's simply not part of your plan to be a championship ball club.

Either way, you hold all the cards.

So keep it up, Ace, continue to ruin all the dreams these little guys can envision in Oxford and Myrtle Beach and Roswell and Gary and Rock Springs...

I've been writing these stories for a long time.

And on the days when I realize how many people have been reached and touched by this particular collection of words, there is a wonderful sensation that continually washes over me.

I know that every night there are kids sitting at the supper table, excitedly telling their families about how their coach let them play second base or catcher or some other position that they've always wanted to play.

Weeks earlier, the same kid would sit quietly, while the family ate dinner, and wonder why he never got a chance to play in the infield or bat in the first inning.

But then his coach found out about *Little Snowman Baseball* and it changed everything.

Overnight!

When these thoughts cross my mind, which they do about a

thousand times every day, I think about all the coaches who came into contact with my thoughts and theories, and then began to ask themselves what in the world had ever motivated them to make such disgusting decisions in the first place.

Yet, ever the optimist, I am absolutely sure that most of those coaches will find a way to make amends.

The best way to help them do that is to let people know what you've learned!

What's done is done.

But Today is a different day!

"If I play the kids that suck then we won't have a chance to win the league this year."

I only repeat that one because I heard the guy say it!

And Ace says things like that in Owensboro and Manhattan and Wheaton and Lemoyne and Lewisburg...

OK Ace, maybe you've rebuffed every single one of my ideas and are still bound and determined to continue coaching your way.

Your thought process is simple, albeit idiotic:

"Ace Junior is obviously the best player on my team, by far. He'll get up to bat four or five times every game. He'll either pitch or play shortstop the entire time. The worst kids will play right field and bat once."

Let's say for the sake of argument that it's gonna be your way or the *highway,* and nothing could change your mind on the matter.

I have an idea.

If one of your kids is only going to get a chance to bat one time in your brilliant scheme, then why not let him bat cleanup in the first inning?

If you keep on treating him the way you have been, then he'll never forget, and forever appreciate, having a chance to bat fourth in the lineup right in the first inning.

He'll be on top of the world for weeks! Why not, Ace?

I can predict the future

There are lots of Little League coaches who are reading this right now. To this point, they've consumed plenty of my valid, sensible, powerful, and passionate *call to action*.

I can see them now. Not physically. But spiritually. They realize that they've been operating in a way that is totally unacceptable. They don't want me to be right, but they know I am.

Here's what happens. They finally throw up their hands and scream,

"Alright! Alright! Alright! No Mas! No Mas! I won't do it anymore!"

The point is that I am never going to stop until they stop! Every day we fix this problem a little more.

Son, He, Him, His could easily morph into Daughter, She, Her, Hers.

I was the only boy in the house with five sisters. I've been around thousands of women and girls. I like women and girls considerably more than I like men and boys.

None of what I do is legislated by the Political Correctness *Institute* anyway, but you probably already know that by now.

Essentially, when I refer to a little boy in Little League, it could just as easily be a little girl.

"Isn't this a great country?"

Here in the USA, we're free to do whatever we wish within the parameters of the law. It's a privilege not always available in all places across the globe.

Often, people take our freedoms for granted, but there are many of us who take full advantage of the opportunity to set our dreams into motion.

Envision any dream you want. Then roll up your sleeves and go attack the goals you've set for yourself. Nobody's gonna stop you.

Kids dream all kinds of things. They aren't limited by reality either. Some want to be Superman or Batman or Spiderman. Others want to be firemen, policemen, teachers, nurses, astronauts, chefs, airplane pilots...

And millions of youngsters decide that they want to be professional ballplayers. They get their moms and dads to sign them up for Little League, and they get so excited!

And then suddenly, a local man in the community becomes his coach and decides right away that the kid isn't good enough, not even worthy of playing for a Little League team.

Ace usually makes that determination in less than thirty seconds too. He observes the fact that the kid can't catch the ball or throw it. And when he bats, he can't hit the ball either.

I guess it never occurred to Ace that he could actually TEACH the kid how to play and COACH him so he'd get better.

That's kinda sorta the job description for a coach, isn't it?

Here's another challenge for Ace that might just wake him up.

Ace, I know that you feel as if you've got an eagle eye. And, for God knows what reason, you also believe that you are a fine coach because you've won some Little League games.

Let's combine both of your supposed skills, and put them to the test. On the first day of practice, look over your little crop of ballplayers and do what you usually do.

Find the littlest guy who exhibits the least amount of talent. He'll be easy for you to spot because you've always been an expert at finding that little boy, and immediately crushing any hopes that he may have had.

But instead of giving him his marching orders to your bench, throw yourself a curve ball. Decide right then and there that you are going to spend extra time with him during the pre-season to help him get better.

And do it with the expressed intention of having him be the leadoff batter for your team in the first game of the season.

What I've just described is called COACHING! And you'll see that when you do coach the proper way, by working with the kids and making each one of them better, it's gonna bring great joy and satisfaction to you in the process. I promise!

The second game of my Little League career was actually more memorable than my first.

Dad told me that instead of wearing pajamas on the night before my second game, he'd seen me climb into bed with my uniform on. The next day at school, my dreams continued on in my mind, and they were all playing out in living color.

Home runs! Strikeouts! Great catches! Anything could happen. I couldn't wait!

Exhausted by the end of the school day, I sat on the couch and threw my ball up in the air again and again, all the while doing my play-by-play of what was going to happen in the game.

I was really pumped up! I was also completely unaware that all of that excitable energy was serving to wear me down and out. Somewhere along in there, I fell fast asleep on the couch.

By the time I woke up, there were only fifteen minutes left until the time the coach had told us to be there! Oh no! What now Batman?

I could always run really fast and I'd need to use every bit of that speed to sprint the three blocks over to the field, and get there on time.

I raced out to the back yard and went to leap over the fence. Somebody had taken one of the sections of the wire fence, and smashed it down so far that it was only about a foot high, and that made it easier for us to climb or jump over it.

But when I jumped, the toe of my back foot caught the top of the fence and I went soaring into the air. And my left knee came crashing down on the edge of a cinder block that had been lying in the yard. My knee cap split wide open!

I was madder than a hornet. I had to get stitched up at the hospital and obviously wasn't able to play that night.

Thinking back, I'm not sure that I've ever missed another baseball game due to illness or injury.

"If your actions inspire others to dream more, learn more, do more and become more, YOU ARE A LEADER" – John Quincy Adams

"Just the facts, ma'am..."

You may need to be of a certain age to recognize that quote, but it was a very funny thing to say back in its day.

Fictional Los Angeles police detective Joe Friday made it famous by saying it in every single episode of the TV drama series called *Dragnet*.

Joe Friday was depicted as a straight-laced, by-the-book cop who interpreted the law in its most literal sense, with no wiggle room whatsoever.

And many people in our society have remembered it, and they've used that phrase to be funny while sharing some credible information with their inner circle of friends and family.

So I thought I'd spend a moment to indoctrinate Ace with *just the facts.*

A varsity high school baseball player has a 5.6 percent chance to play college baseball. And that same varsity high school player has a 0.015 percent chance to make it to the big leagues.

I read that on an NCAA website one day, and the writer likened the chances of a high school player getting to the majors as being about the same odds as a thief guessing your PIN number on the first try.

Pretty sobering numbers.

Ace, I'm not saying that Ace Junior couldn't wind up defying those odds. In fact, I root for Junior just as hard as I do for every other kid on earth.

But those statistics alone should make you realize that your job in Little League is to simply teach all of them what you know, and have fun with your little guys in the process.

If a High School varsity baseball player goes to the big leagues 0.015% of the time, what do you think the chances are that a Little Leaguer will make it to the majors?

We really need to educate these coaches by making darn sure they realize that Used to Be's don't count anymore.

It's certainly a wonderful time to create a fresh new message that Ace can easily understand.

We can reinforce upon him what Thomas Jefferson said so many years ago, "*All men are created equal.*"

When you get down to brass tacks, that's the only thing Ace really needs to know.

It's heartwarming to know how many of these formerly abusive coaches are now being reeled in by a boatload of newly-educated parents and other interested parties!

And this is happening in so many new places like Mansfield and Olympia and Virginia Beach and Houston and Memphis...

Ace, I really don't care who you are, what you know, where you've been, or what you've accomplished.

You are merely a Little League coach, and you are not a very good one if Ace Junior is given preferential treatment for any reason.

I know it's hard in the beginning to realize that your team could survive, and possibly even thrive, during a time when Ace Junior is sitting on the pine for a few innings every game.

These kids are in elementary school for crying out loud! Maybe that thought alone should bring you to your senses.

Give all the kids an equal chance. Ace Junior is not more important than another kid. Put Junior on the bench for as many innings as the benchwarmers that you are already sitting now.

It's awfully hard to do, isn't it?

But, it sure hasn't been hard for you to put other people's kids on the bench for most of the game.

Why is that?

Our playoff opponents had already crushed us in both games that we played against them during the regular season.

One of my players came to me before the game, to let me know that a kid on the opposing team had taunted him all day because of how they'd walloped the living daylights out of us in both of the games during the season.

A couple things came to my mind right away, but I didn't share either one of them with my baby-faced ballplayer.

Instead I told him the biblical story of the famous duel between David and Goliath. David was barely half the size of Goliath, but surprised the big oaf by using a rock from a slingshot that struck him right in the head, and knocked him out cold.

Then I reminded my little guy that the score of every game begins with a 0-0 tie. And I added, *"We've been playing great baseball lately. They should be worried about us, instead of the other way around!"*

I winked at him and sent him back to the dugout. He probably wasn't completely convinced, but he knew we were gonna have fun either way.

The first time we played them, they beat us by twenty five runs. It was only our second game of the year and we were still finding our way.

My schedule didn't allow me to be in attendance for that game, so Gage called to tell me about it. During the call, he told me that he felt terrible because we had got beaten so badly.

I reassured him that I could care less which team won, or lost, a Little League baseball game, much less what the final margin of victory may have been.

82

We played them for a second time at mid-season and got hammered again, but it wasn't nearly as lopsided as the first time around.

At that time, our record was two wins and five losses, so the only way that we'd play them again was if we somehow found a way to make it to the playoffs.

That seemed like a longshot at the time.

I also remembered something from my junior year in High School, when we had what many of us believed to be a state championship caliber baseball team.

Our record was 34-3 when we headed into the playoffs and we had crushed everybody in our path all year long.

We were also very fortunate. We had the opportunity to play our games in a minor league baseball stadium with eight thousand seats. We had dressing rooms, showers, and training rooms at our disposal.

We even had outfield fences like the ones they have in the big leagues! Plus we'd play our games early in the evening just before the minor league games would begin.

This meant that we had lots of extra people watching us out on the diamond. These were real baseball fans—paying customers!—who infused a fresh, new energy into the ballpark.

I always believed that we played better baseball simply because we wanted to strut our stuff and shine for them. I think those bonus fans were at least partly responsible for our success.

We were getting dressed in the locker room before our first game in the tournament. It was against a team from the next town over that we'd already played four times that season.

We had beaten them every time, but I remember thinking about how well those kids played, and how competitive they always were. They finished up their season at 22-13.

Throughout the locker room, I kept hearing my teammates crowing about how great our team was and how we had beaten our rivals every time we played them.

The more they boasted, the more it sounded to me that they figured it was a foregone conclusion that the ballgame was going to be a rout, and we'd be advancing to the next round with ease.

Oh, it was a rout all right.

We got pounded like a big bass drum that night—14-3! And the kids from our neighboring town were the ones who ended up being the team advancing on to the sectionals.

Even before that game began, I had a sneaky suspicion deep down in my bones causing me to sense that an upset like that was brewing.

That's why they play the games...

I didn't change one darn thing when my little guys got into the playoffs.

They were playing excellent baseball with great confidence in one another. I think we had to win our last five games in order to qualify for the tournament. And we did.

So when we made our way into the post-season, it remained business as usual for our team. Every one of the kids played lots of baseball, and the places where they batted in the lineup was still determined by the order that they showed up to play.

It meant that every one of them would have a chance to make a big play in the field, or drive home the winning run, or strike out a batter to end the game.

My methods and philosophies were unquestionably different than most people had ever seen before.

But I knew that I had created a way to squash the sickening

prevailing sentiment that has poisoned Little Leagues for three quarters of a century.

Basically, we loved to win like anybody else. But it didn't mean a hill of beans to us if we didn't.

We were providing our team with an environment where they could play, learn, develop, grow, and enjoy themselves.

A doctrine of fairness and open lines of communication worked extremely well for the team—for all of us.

Doesn't that sound ridiculous? Am I the world's biggest weirdo? Am I the guy from Namby-Pamby Land prancing around looking to create Little League utopia?

Yeah, you keep thinking that.

Maybe you think I was a little shrimp, who had to sit on the bench all the time in Little League, so now I'm trying to exact some measure of revenge here.

Think again. I've spent a lifetime playing sports. Baseball. Basketball. Wrestling. Track and Field. Football. I played them all.

I was also a Sergeant in the Army, a 2nd Class Petty Officer in the Navy and a Staff Sergeant in the Air Force.

Add in the fact that I was a ferocious boxer who roamed the Mediterranean, Caribbean and North Atlantic Seas knocking out guys who came from anywhere, and everywhere around the globe.

In fact, I won my first 23 fights. Anybody they stood up in front of me got hammered from pillar to post.

Bottom line: I'm tougher than a two dollar steak.

But, believe me, none of this is about me. It's about abhorrent adult behavior that's been allowed to continue forever and a year. And it makes me madder than a hornet every time I think about it!

And I think about it every single day, whether I'm on the Las Vegas Strip or talking about it on the phone. And I'll continue to do this every time the sun comes up, for as long as I'm drawing breath.

It's these *win at all* costs attitudes, prevailing in far too many places, that have always been so worrisome to me.

Our first post-season game was set to begin, and I chose to send a young boy named Kyle out to the mound to be our starting pitcher.

And Kyle had never even thrown one pitch in a game in his life!

At the first practice of the season, I made deals with all of my players. We agreed that each and every one of them would get a chance to play every position on the field that they wanted to play.

And that included having the opportunity to be our pitcher.

But getting that chance to pitch for us did come with one

important stipulation. Each of them had to prove to me that they had the strength and ability to throw the ball over the plate, on a consistent basis.

I didn't want kids trying to pitch if they weren't able to throw strikes. The agreement was that I would warm them up myself whenever they believed they were ready.

And it was awfully cool to watch our whole team standing there rooting for every one of their teammates who were auditioning to pitch!

No matter how long it took them to be able to do it, once they had passed my test, they'd be on the mound for us in the very next game.

Kyle couldn't get the hang of it for most of the season, but he kept on trying. He really wanted to pitch, and every player on the team was pulling for him to finally get his chance to do it.

Sure enough, one week before the playoffs, he tried again and this time Kyle threw enough pitches either in the strike zone, or close enough, and he was rewarded with his trip to the pitcher's mound.

I was more than happy to hold up my end of the bargain. He was so fired up!

I also realize that only about one coach in a million would have sent Kyle out to the mound for a playoff game with absolutely no experience.

It was just a matter of me honoring a deal by following through on my promise to him.

I could hear a few little whispers throughout the bleachers when the game began. But nobody approached me wondering why I would do such a thing. And I knew they wouldn't.

Prior to the season, I had met with all the parents and shared my visions and philosophies. I gave them plenty of time to take their sons and put them on other teams if they didn't agree with me.

I made sure they knew the things I planned on doing, along with the reasons I was going to do them. I explained that wins and losses meant absolutely nothing to me.

My platform was to teach their kids, have fun with them, and make sure that every one of them was going to have plenty of chances to get better.

Hanging a championship banner was not among my priorities, and I made absolutely sure that the parents and guardians understood me in no uncertain terms.

Not one of them challenged me then, so there certainly was no reason to expect me to change my stripes now.

Kyle did struggle a bit, as he gave up four runs in the first inning. He also struck out the last two batters on six pitches! I was so proud of him and all of his teammates backslapped him when the team came back into the dugout.

When we came up to bat in the fifth inning, we were trailing 10-2 so we had lots of work to do to try and catch up.

But suddenly that fifth inning turned into my favorite inning of baseball in my whole life! Magic unfolded right before my eyes.

With two outs and runners on second and third, Kyle hit a high bouncing ball that barely eluded the outstretched glove of the pitcher for an infield hit and one run crossed the plate. Billy steered a single into right field, making the score 10-4 with two runners on base and two outs.

Nathan walked and Benjamin came up with the bases loaded. He smashed the first pitch down the left field line and it went all the way to the fence in the corner. When the smoke had cleared, Benjamin was sliding into third base with a three-run triple.

Now, it was 10-7.

They brought in a new pitcher and he walked the first batter he faced. And guess who came up to bat?

Johnny Stone! My little STONEMAN!!!

Remember now, here was a kid who'd never even gotten one hit in nearly four years of playing baseball. And now, there he was standing in the batter's box representing the tying run in our playoff game!

Could it be that this was the stage he'd been waiting for the whole time? He wasn't scared. In fact, I could tell that he was excited.

And then he did something that I will never forget for the rest of my days.

He clobbered the first pitch into the right center field gap and it bounced off the fence on one hop! It knocked in both runners and when Johnny slid into second base, I could see the biggest smile you could ever imagine on his little face.

It was pure delight!

Johnny popped up quickly after his slide and excitedly clapped his hands together three or four times. I saw him spin his head around to see exactly where he'd hit that ball. He scalded it!

The kid, who was forced to play baseball against his wishes, had just created a marvelous lifetime memory, not just for himself, but for ME too!

We didn't win the game. We were eliminated that night. We had a little rally going in the sixth inning, but it fizzled out.

The game was over and so was the season. It was a terrific year that those kids will remember throughout their lives.

And I will always remember it too. It has more than its share of staying power

In fact I came very close to calling this volume, *Little Johnny Baseball.*

I have even proof!

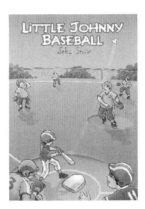

He meant that much to me.

They all did.

A lot of coaching behavior that I've witnessed is downright scary.

Grown men treating the Little league landscape as if it were a Texas Death match is something that has bewildered me all my life.

Most of the guys who behave that way are simply copying what they've seen before. There usually isn't much creativity going on when dealing with Ace and his crew.

These coaches are not necessarily mean, nor are they stupid. What they are is unaware.

That's where I come in. I take them from being unaware to being COMPLETELY AWARE!

They believe that they're doing something special for their own children. They like being able to be a part of their kid's lives in this way.

These coaches have just never been exposed to the thoughts and ideas contained on these pages.

But now Ace is being exposed to them in Corpus Christi and Bloomington and Fairfield and Dearborn and Santa Barbara...

Ace is 33 years old. And the father of one of his players is 33 years old too.

They both have a son on the team who is eleven-years- old. And both kids have played in all twelve of the team's games during the season.

But that's precisely where the similarities end.

Ace Junior plays all six innings in every game that the team plays, whereas the son of that other 33-year-old father plays for only one inning in each of the games.

Allow me to reveal some simple math here that will help to clearly illustrate this point:

We've established that Ace Junior didn't sit on the bench for even one inning during the year. That adds up to zero innings spent on the bench for the entire season.

Meanwhile, the other kid in this example sat in the dugout for sixty innings!

ZERO INNINGS versus SIXTY INNINGS! And why do I feel the need to use capital letters here?

Maybe it's because I know that Ace has never even noticed the staggering disparity in those numbers.

Is this just some amazing statistical anomaly?!

Amazing?

No, it is not amazing.

It's criminal. That's what it is!

Two different eleven-year-olds, on the same team, with a SIXTY INNING disparity in playing time?

How in God's good holy name can Ace possibly justify doing that?

And doesn't anybody notice this kind of terrorist activity?!!

Yes, some folks do notice it and recognize what's going on, but they'd rather not rock the boat. They'd prefer not to get involved.

In most cases, these people might like to help, but they're simply not sure what they can do so they just keep their thoughts to themselves.

The sad truth is that most people don't notice at all. But I'll tell you somebody who definitely does notice.

It's that group of kids who are banished to the bench, and forced to sit and wonder why Ace chose them to sit and watch the games from the dugout for SIXTY INNINGS in one season.

These little guys are keenly aware of what's going on, and the truth is that they have never had any options available to them.

Until now!

I've always been a different kind of cat.

There's never been a time when I've felt the need to succumb to any of the societal norms.

So it sure wouldn't surprise me one bit if you might be thinking something like this right now:

"Jake is a nut-job. He talks about all kinds of crazy stuff. But he is making some pretty solid and valid points here. And I can see why he communicates with us the way that he does because he's right. None of this is ever gonna stop until somebody gently force-feeds this information to these ignorant coaches!"

Is that fair? Has that been part of your mindset while reading along today?

First and foremost, these guys are not now, nor will they ever be, volunteering their time so that they can carry on the heartwarming tradition of Little League baseball in their communities.

Believe me, this is NOT about their love for Little League baseball at all. They could care less about Little League baseball!

The fact of the matter is that 99% of these guys aren't qualified to coach at any other level anyway! This is their chance for one personal shining moment.

You'll see that the length of time that they coach Little League will coincide EXACTLY with the amount of time that their little Ace Juniors play in the league.

Once Junior is no longer eligible to play in Little League, Ace will immediately conclude his coaching reign of terror and never again go to another Little League game until he has grandchildren.

During the period of time that he does coach, Ace will consistently put Ace Junior up on a pedestal, giving him the ultimate star treatment which includes perks and benefits that Junior definitely never earned or deserved.

Meanwhile, Ace will unwittingly extinguish the dreams of some of his own players, by continually making the same grotesque decisions every time his team plays a game.

At every one of his games, Ace has a small group of kids sitting in his dugout watching the game rather than playing in it.

No matter what length of time that he coaches, Ace's blatant nepotism will wind up being his only legacy.

This has gotta stop!

And it's gonna stop RIGHT HERE and RIGHT NOW!

As you no doubt already realize, I'm awfully serious about helping these formerly helpless and unprotected youngsters.

I know I've made it abundantly clear that I'm thrilled to be driving this ship.

I'm sure that my unwavering passion isn't difficult to spot.

Whether you're reading these words for the first time, or you've heard me share them with you before, *Little Snowman Baseball* is a topic that I talk about every single day of my life.

Both of my dad's parents lived for a very long time, with each of them soaring well past ninety years old. Apparently, the life-lines run long in my family.

Using their ages as a barometer, it's possible that I may only be about two-thirds of the way through my own life. I've already established that I personally touch 36,000 people every year.

So if I were to live for thirty more years, I will be personally meeting a total of 1,080,000 people—more than a MILLION of you all by myself!

And I don't just touch, I also energize people just like you. And together we will reach tens of millions of people, just in the course of living our daily lives.

Think about this, I have guaranteed my own happiness for every one of my remaining days. I am a person with a definitive purpose and I live my life like my hair's on fire.

Operating with the passion of a hundred men, I find myself to be completely in tune with the universe.

Every day, the world gets better because of me.

And YOU!!!

When each year begins, Ace Junior will probably be a little bit more prepared for the season than some of his teammates.

This is true because Ace is very excited about the upcoming season, and he gets himself ready by taking Junior outside for some batting and fielding practice.

He gets out in the yard with the boy as often as he can.

But what Ace fails to realize is that not every player on his team will be coming from a household where an option like that is available.

Some of the little guys that show up will be playing baseball for the first time. There will be other kids who have never even played a game of catch before. That's the whole reason they signed up for baseball. They wanted to learn how to play baseball!

Some of them will be returning from the previous year, and they'll be praying that they won't have to sit on Ace's bench all season long again.

Not to worry, Ace is right there at the ready, making sure that the youngster stays good and frustrated again.

We gotta stop this guy folks!!!

And we're stopping him cold in Grand Forks and Tucson and Green Bay and Hialeah and Charleston...

Our pregame fielding practice was very unusual too.

Nobody had ever seen it done my way before. And, of course, that came as no surprise to anybody either .

If you've ever watched the customary Little League pregame infield practice, you've seen that Ace will deploy four infielders around the diamond, and then mundanely hit routine ground balls to each fielder from his left to right.

He starts by hitting one on a couple of easy bounces to the third baseman, and then to the shortstop, and then to the second baseman, and round and round they go. I'm sure you get the idea.

The kids stand there waiting for the ball to be hit to them, and they know exactly when Ace is going to hit it to them too!

It is completely scripted . Routine. Boring. Useless.

Any fool could see that. Do the baseballs come at you in a rehearsed fashion like that once the game starts? Of course not!

That's why when we conducted our infield practice, we did it in a way that would get ALL the players on the team ready for the game!

My players were constantly on the move. Every one of them rotated through different defensive positions all over the field.

A kid could begin the drill playing second base and wind up out in left field, by the time we finished up.

Defensive fielding positions in baseball are numbered 1 through 9. Those numbers are based on where a defensive player is stationed on the field. For instance, in the scorebook, the second baseman is identified as a 4, the center fielder is an 8, and so forth.

At any point during the drill, I might holler, "*OK, everybody add 3 to whatever position you are in now, and you've eight seconds to get over there.*"

In that example, the shortstop—6—would run out to right field—9. The catcher—2—would now become the third baseman—5.

It was simple math, but they all had to be on their toes.

All nine of them would be running all over the place. And they wouldn't be dilly-dallying either! They'd all sprint to their new positions, and get there in plenty of time.

Then I'd hit the ball wherever in the heck I felt like hitting it. I knew that every one of them would get themselves in fielding position and be ready to make the play.

The funny thing was that we did this before every game we played. And rest assured that my little guys were putting on a show in the process! Everybody stopped to watch them!

My Little Leaguers were doing something that nobody had ever seen before. And they had more fun than a barrel of monkeys doing it.

None of my kids were ever plugged into one specific position on the field. Nobody was just a shortstop or just a centerfielder or just a catcher.

They were all little ballplayers learning how to play baseball.

It didn't take forever and a year to teach them the value of being versatile either. Like everything else we did, it was simply a matter of teamwork and hustle and wanting to be a better player.

The cool thing is that any one of my players who choose, or have already chosen, to coach Little League baseball will make their team's infield practice look just like the ones of their youth.

It's truly OK to have fun with every kid on the team instead of just members of your own tribe.

When my kids were little, I taught them, *"All you can do is the best you can do."*

I probably didn't make that up. More than likely, I heard it somewhere before. But it has to be true, doesn't it? If you do your best and it isn't good enough, what else could you have done? You tried your best.

If you fall short of your goals after giving your best effort, there are only a few things that might have changed the outcome.

You may have had the best intentions, but perhaps you didn't have the best knowledge, information, or training to achieve your desired result.

This reminds me of the old saying, *"If you don't know where you're going, any road will get you there."*

I've seen a commercial on television promoting foster parenthood. It's quite comical in nature, as it shows the new foster dad making mistake after mistake while trying to teach his kids how to do things.

In the end, the announcer tells the viewers that you don't have to be perfect to be a dad because there are thousands of kids who would be happy to have you just the way you are.

To me, that's a beautiful sentiment. Kids just need your time, love, and attention. They need to know that they matter to somebody.

And isn't that really the only job of a Little League coach?

If Ace framed his methodology around the foster parent concept, I believe he'd be much more effective, and many of the atrocities he's committing now would just float away.

I'm not certain what the requirements are to become a foster parent. Surely there must be a criminal background check and other ways to ensure safety for all concerned.

On the other hand, you wouldn't need to pass exams in Science or Mathematics or History to meet the requirements.

Meanwhile, Ace doesn't need to qualify at all. He doesn't need to pass a test on strategy, philosophy, or the history of the game. He signs up, he gets a whistle and then gets a bunch of kids to coach.

And just like the foster parent, he doesn't need to be perfect!

Like in so many other parts of life, it all starts with attitude. If a coach takes on his volunteer role with the mindset of showing his kids that he is rooting for them, all of them, then he is already an excellent coach!

He might not even know third base from right field when he begins, but he can easily find people to help him figure things out.

In other words, if he doesn't know the sport, he wouldn't have any bad habits to break! He'd be learning right alongside the kids.

Essentially, the job is to show interest and enthusiasm anytime you are with your players. Learn together. Get better together. Try your best, and be your best! It doesn't need to be any more complicated than that.

I remember Benjamin playing on his first team. The entire emphasis of that coaching staff was on winning and they customarily did win their games. It wasn't unusual for them to win by as many as thirty or forty runs! Crazy!

Who is having fun in ballgames with those kinds of scores? The spirit of competition was totally absent.

And yet, Benjamin never started a game, never played anywhere other than right field, and always batted in the last spot in the lineup.

At the end of the season, he was awarded a trophy that was almost as big as he was, and he knew he hadn't done anything to warrant such a prize.

As the next season was approaching, Benjamin told his mother that he didn't want to play baseball anymore. He was nervous about telling me his decision because he knew I was planning on coaching that season. She asked me not to be mad at him.

Mad at him? Not a chance!

When he approached me, I told him, *"If I had gotten treated the way that you were treated last year, I wouldn't want to play anymore either."*

He really wanted to play and did end up changing his mind later that month. And when he returned to the baseball field, he became a holy terror!

He hammered home runs fifty feet over the fences. He once struck out eleven kids in a row, or was it twelve?

Here was a kid who was completely overlooked by a coaching

99

staff that was hell bent on winning their Little League championship and getting trophies.

Once again, my firm belief is that the only job of a Little League coach is to make the time interesting and fun enough, so the kids would want to sign up again the following year.

Let each kid make the choice as to whether they want to keep on playing or not.

Don't make it for them!

When you show favoritism to certain players on a Little League team, you are not doing anything other than stunting the growth of other little kids with big dreams.

And why would you do that? You wouldn't knowingly do that, would you?

Remember that if each one of those kids is given the same opportunity, the same instruction, the same attention, and the same opportunities to play, then it's gonna be a rewarding experience for the whole squad.

Why is that so hard to understand?

Bo was running late one night.

He owned a restaurant and worked seventy-five to eighty hours a week. He had to get his son over to his Little League game and found himself in a great big hurry to get everything done before he headed out to the field.

Always with a million things on his mind, Bo found the glove and the hat and the uniform. He put a bat and a couple of bottles of water on the front seat.

It was his week to bring the sodas so he ran down to the basement and grabbed a couple of cases. He shoved them into a cooler and filled it with ice and slid it into the bed of his truck.

As usual, Bo had taken care of every single detail on the fly. He was very proud of himself. He fired up the engine and got to the field exactly at the time the coach had requested.

He had beaten the clock again.

But as it turns out, Bo did forget one thing in his haste. Bo forgot to bring his kid!

Benjamin asked me a question many years ago and, to this day, I've never been able to give him a proper answer.

It was a simple *Yes* or *No* baseball question. And he was asking the question to the guy that probably knew more about baseball, and its history, than anybody else in our town—ME!

He was a nine-year-old who was headed up to bat for the first time in his life. His cap was too big. The giant helmet that he'd selected could have spun right around on his head like a top.

The waist of his pants was so big that two Benjamins could have fit inside them. And the pant legs were so long that they dangled underneath his little spikes.

And the bases were all loaded up for him!

Suffice it to say, he didn't race up to home plate with a boatload of confidence. He turned to look at me a couple of times on his way to the plate, and got a knowing wink in return.

We talked about baseball all the time and he loved it. Now was his first chance to swing his bat in game action. He stood outside the batter's box and took a couple of disjointed swings. He stepped up to the plate and it was *Game On*!

The pitcher was nearly twice as big as little Benjamin. He was throwing the ball really hard and wasn't throwing many pitches over the plate either. His last pitch to the previous batter had ricocheted high off the backstop! Yikes!

That would make any hitter uneasy coming up to bat, but just imagine if it were the first time you were ever standing in a batter's box!

Sure enough, the first pitch blazed inside—hard and low—and the fastball hit Benjamin right in the middle of his left thigh.

He really showed me something because he just dropped his bat and hopped all the way down to first base, as the runner from third base trotted home and scored.

Tears were probably flowing through his eyes, but nobody saw them and that included me. The coaches and a few parents came onto the field to check him out medically and he was fine.

Now, how do you write that in the scorebook? HBP—Hit by Pitch. RBI—Run Batted In.

Over the next couple days, his leg turned every color of the rainbow, as the bruise deepened, and then healed.

And it was during that time when he asked me,

"Dad, am I the first player in history to be hit by a pitch and drive in a run in my first ever at bat?"

Hmmm.

Sometimes while we are watching a ballgame, the announcer will tell us that Sammy Smith was batting .355 in afternoon games, that were played on Astroturf, on a Tuesday, when there were more than 18,000 fans in the park, during the month of June, while the sun was peeking through the clouds.

They have stats about everything—many more than we would ever need.

Yet, to this day, we still don't officially know if Benjamin made history in his first career at bat!

I loved hosting sports talk radio programs all across the USA.

I was very happy on the air, and audiences must have liked my cheerfulness and style because our ratings were always very high, regardless of where I happened to be on the radio dial.

Generally we dominated the local market.

I enjoyed staying on top of every sports development, so I could inform and entertain my audiences. It was my great pleasure to serve in that capacity.

"Do something you love and never have to work a day in your life."

Brimming with unrivaled confidence, I did something that no sportscaster had ever done. On Wednesdays, I only allowed women to call in. No male callers at all.

I have five sisters, and I know first-hand that women can understand the games just as easily as any man could.

Everybody enjoyed Wednesday nights in those days.

The best calls were when wives or girlfriends called in to quote their partner on subjects that pertained to sports. *"Jake, my husband told me this, that or the other thing. Is that really true?"*

About half the time, I would mock their husband and make fun of him—tongue in cheek, of course—or I might even say, "*Did he really tell you that? Put that clown on the phone!"* Everybody had a good time. Wednesday nights were often the best shows of the week.

One Wednesday night, a woman called in and said, "*I have a bone to pick with you, Buster Brown*." I knew I was gonna love what she said next because of the playfulness that was clearly evident in her voice.

She told me a story about how she had come home on Tuesday night with three bags of groceries. She parked in the garage and then tried to go through the door leading to the kitchen.

As it turned out, the door was locked, and she'd left her keys in the car. She banged on the door, in the hopes that her husband would hear her and let her in.

But, as she tells it, her husband wouldn't come to the door until my show went to a commercial! Huh?! I told her to put him on the phone right away, and I playfully let him have it for a minute or two.

He took his medicine in the spirit in which it was intended, and did a great job of being my straight man. I ended the call by telling him,

"I'm not starting one of those Eastern religions here, I'm just talking about sports!"

That one made our annual Christmas party highlight reel and, to this day, it makes me laugh every time I think about it.

The sobering news is realizing that far too many coaches have turned the Little League landscape into *"One of those Eastern religions",* and it bothers me to the ends of the earth.

My belief is that sports are to be thoroughly enjoyed by all who play them, and not just on the nights when our favorite teams happen to triumph!

"In a gentle way, you can shake the world" – Gandhi

Your home life probably has a family component that comes with it.

Household members come and go to work and school and other activities. There's food on the table and the bills get paid.

You've always loved baseball, and your son told you that he'd like to learn to play too. The natural thing would be for you to coach his Little League team. It's going to work out perfectly. You get home from work at 4:30, and the games don't start until six o'clock.

Before the season starts, you take your little guy out in the yard and play catch with him almost every day. When time permits, you take him to the batting cages. It's pretty slow going at first but, with practice, he starts getting better.

In your expert opinion, you believe that Ace Junior should be the pitcher on the team because you know he'll be able to take charge and lead your squad to the top of the standings.

Now, let's spend a moment in another household in your town. A little boy watches baseball every day. It is his sanctuary because he isn't in a happy home. His dad is a drunk and rarely comes home. When he does, he spends most of the time yelling at his mom.

His mom copes by taking drugs that help her to forget about the pain in her life. Seldom is there enough food, so this hungry little guy spends his free time thinking about baseball. One day he hopes to play for the big-league team in his area.

He asks his mom for weeks and weeks to sign him up for baseball. He's never even thrown a ball yet, but he knows he would learn fast. When he shows up for that first practice, he's the happiest kid on that field. It's his dream being realized.

When the season starts, Ace Junior gets right out onto that pitching mound and he hits leadoff in the batting order too. Ace made sure that Junior is all set up to be the star of the show.

Meanwhile, the other little guy gets a chance to sit on the bench while the other kids play. He watches and waits for his turn to play. But he doesn't get his chance to play until the last inning of the game.

Does any of that make any sense? No it doesn't!

And it's gonna happen again tonight unless we stop it.

It's Eminent Domain. From sea to shining sea. Actually it crosses all the seas!

It's a runaway train, a wild mustang, a raging fire. But we're stopping this cycle of rampant ignorance, one coach at a time.

Hey Ace, whatcha gonna do when we come for you?

I ask you that because we are coming for you in Dubuque and Billings and Nashua and Silver Springs and Lincoln ...

The coach stands in front of his new Little League team and asks them a couple of questions.

"How many of you want to play baseball?" Every hand goes up.

"How many of you want to learn baseball?" Every hand raises again.

"OK guys, starting today we're a team. We are going to play together, and learn together. We're going to practice every time

we get a chance. And we're going to get better and better, all season long. Now let's get started. Let's go get 'em."

It's a great way for kids to start the season. They want to be part of something. It's a lot of fun to teach kids how to win by showing them how to play better and smarter.

All of them.

Every Little Leaguer who ever signed up to play is a special and unique member of the World of Baseball.

Ace, these youngsters are in the same World of Baseball as you. And all of them are most certainly special and unique.

You, on the other hand, are no more than a carbon copy of hundreds of thousands of other non-thinking adults who have treated other people's children like doormats for generations.

Ace, allowing you to make talent assessments is utterly preposterous in the first place. What earned you the right to make them in the first place?!

It's over fellas. There's no place to run and hide anymore.

And that's because we've got boots on the ground in Charlotte and Hampton Roads and Mexico City and Blue Mounds and Woodstock...

Benjamin was much different than me in so many ways, including his ability to mull things over.

He knew that he hadn't gotten a fair shake in his first year. He only got up to bat about twenty times for the whole season, yet there were kids on his own team that had seventy or more chances to hit.

No exaggeration.

One night that Winter, he said to me, "*Hey Dad, I thought of a whole bunch of places where I could get hit by a pitch that wouldn't even hurt!*" And he started pointing them out!

My thought on the subject was completely different than his, "*Hey little buddy, why on earth are you thinking about getting hit by pitches?*"

"*Benjamin, I want you to remember something. You get to bring that great big bat up to home plate and all the pitcher has is that little baseball. You are the one that's holding the hammer!*"

He looked at me, and I could see the light go on in his eyes. He clearly understood the point that I was making. And it was fascinating to see how confident he became in just that one split-second in time!

He couldn't wait to swing a baseball bat again! Hurry up Springtime!

Those are special times in a parent's life when you can enjoy how good it feels to coach—and to love at the same time.

Once when the kids showed up for practice, there were no balls or bats to be found anywhere.

We didn't play baseball that afternoon.

Instead we flew kites. I brought enough for all of them, and I was able to watch the magic unfold when twelve Little Leaguers gleefully ran all over that field for an hour.

It was another piece of proof that they were all just kids who wanted to play together. It was beautiful to see.

I wonder if Ace would have made his benchwarmers sit in the dugout with their kites, and watch as Ace Junior was the Leader of the Band on the field.

Just wonderin'...

I think that it's more fun to root for a little guy than it is to root for a big guy.

Heck, he doesn't even need to be on your team. Look at his little face and his determination. It's a beautiful thing!

It's OK, Ace. You can root for a little guy no matter what color uniform he is wearing! You can cheer for all the kids, on all the teams in the league.

Let the little guy play and watch him as he learns new things from you. When you teach him, and show patience, he'll always get better if you give him a chance to play.

"This is the song that never ends,

it goes on and on my friends.

Some people started singing it

not knowing what it was

and they'll continue singing it forever just because,

This is the song that never ends

it goes on and on my friends.

Some people started singing it

not knowing what it was

and they'll continue singing it forever just because

This is the song that never ends..."

And in a nutshell, that's my entire platform, isn't it?! It's a silly song, but it sums up my position on this subject perfectly.

One song that's not so silly is the *Sounds of Silence* by Simon and Garfunkel. One slice of those amazing lyrics sounded like this,

"People writing songs that voices never shared."

My song has *voices* with brand new ones joining in every day! And these stories are being told in loud whispers behind every rock and bush in this world!

We don't need to raise our voices at all. This message works no matter where we set the volume.

The *Little Snowman Baseball* song will be sung today, tomorrow, and every day thereafter until the Earth is no longer in business.

I looked up the definition of conniving today.

I'd always had an idea of what the word conniving might have meant, but if I'd been pressed on the matter, I really didn't know the actual definition.

Now I do.

It means, *"given to or involved in conspiring to do something immoral, illegal or harmful."*

Do you think that Ace is conniving when he has kids on his team who spend the bulk of their time on the bench, while Ace Junior plays in every inning of every game?

I think it is conniving behavior because I know it's harmful and has long lasting effects.

Can you imagine a ten-year-old being subjected to totally unnecessary harm by a guy who has absolutely no credentials to be making any such decisions in the first place?

Just out of curiosity...

Do you think that there are any benchwarmers in *Snowball Heaven?*

My guess is that there are no benchwarmers in *Snowball Heaven.*

But if you want to watch some benchwarmers, you can come and see them wasting away in Little League dugouts in Littleton and Jackson and Baton Rouge and Fargo and Champaign...

Little League is NOT a developmental league.

OK Ace, do NOT try shoveling me that big bag of crap about how you are grooming a kid for upcoming seasons because he is younger or smaller than the others. Nothing could be more foolish.

Start with this:

Let's say Ace Junior is twelve and one of his teammates is ten. So Ace decides that because Junior is bigger and older, he will play this season and the other kid will get his chance to play, in subsequent seasons, later on down the line.

But the fact of the matter is that on the very same day that Ace Junior finishes playing Little League baseball, Ace is gonna be all done with Little League baseball too.

Immediately!

Ace will absolutely not stick around to continue the supposed development of any of those players that he benched, under the guise of returning to coach them in upcoming seasons.

What Ace always ends up leaving behind is a group of kids who spent entire seasons sitting on his bench, due to his disgraceful, nepotism-laced tactics.

And those little guys that he leaves behind can be found in Juneau and Portland and Colorado Springs and Biddeford and San Antonio...

"My name is Jerry Brennan and we are now ready to proceed with today's deposition."

"Present in the room are Inspector Frederick Jones, from the Little League Home Office in Williamsport, Pennsylvania, Deputy Commissioner Arnold Martin, from our Little League state headquarters, and Coach Ace Williams of the Cardinals, from our Burlington Central Little League."

"Also present is our videographer, Luther Walsh, along with Jake Snow—the Snowman in Vegas—who will be conducting the questioning of Mr. Ace Williams."

Jake Snow: *"Thank you, Jerry. Good Morning Ace. Let me begin by asking if you are in possession of scorebooks that prove that there were four separate players on your Little League team who sat on the bench for 36 innings each during this past season?"*

Ace Williams: *"Yes I am."*

Jake Snow: *"Does the same documentation unequivocally reflect and, further substantiate, that your son—AKA Ace Junior—did not sit on the bench for even one inning during the season?"*

Ace Williams: *"Yes it does."*

Jake Snow: *"Do you further understand that the resulting mathematics clearly indicate that those other four players sat for a cumulative 144 innings while Ace Junior sat for zero innings?"*

Ace Williams: "Yes I do."

Jake Snow: *"And how would you justify your actions? Can you please give me a breakdown on how you came to make these playing time decisions regarding five different eleven-year-old baseball players?"*

Ace Williams: *"Well, Ace Junior is a fantastic player—head and shoulders better than those other four kids combined. Anybody would be able to easily see that."*

Jake Snow: *"So Ace, would it be fair for me to assume that you will be going forward with an Insanity defense?"*

Little League coaches seem to enjoy copying the actions of the men who manage ball clubs in the major leagues.

Most of these guys would prefer to only send their nine *best* Little Leaguers onto that field and never have to worry about how those other kids, who were wasting away on the bench, felt about sitting there.

But Ace, along with many of his Little League brethren, is forced to spend part of his valuable game preparation time devising plans on how to split up playing time between four or five of his little benchwarmers.

Ace isn't always in agreement with what he finds to be harsh and restrictive rules requiring him to play all of his players in every game.

Playing his benchwarmers frequently causes problems for Ace, especially when one of them strikes out or makes an error. If Ace had his way, those kids would never have played in the game at all.

So due to the mandates forcing him to give all of them a chance to play, Ace has to be creative. He somehow has to find ways to rotate those benchwarmers into less crucial positions on the diamond.

Usually that means divvying up time for these bad ballplayers to stand out in right or left field for just a few innings each. The way Ace has it figured is that he has done it in a fashion that gives his team their best chance to win.

Basically he uses the same type of game plan in every game of the season. He starts out by deciding that Billy and Joey and Lenny can split the game playing two innings each in right field.

And that leaves Jackie and Myron to play three innings apiece in left field.

Ace's careful construction of these lineups are of the utmost importance, and the decisions that he makes are crucial to the success of his Little League team.

Imagine the pressure involved?

There are five kids on Ace's own team who've somehow managed to create tremendous frustration for him!

These kids have caused Ace all of this consternation simply because they had the nerve to sign up to play on his Little League team. And they should have known that there were no available positions for them to play on Ace's squad.

So whenever Ace feels the urge, and then acts on the temptation, to operate in the exact same way every single time he makes out his lineup cards, he does so with a total disregard for the wants and wishes of elementary school children.

Thank the Lord up in heaven that he doesn't have to include Ace Junior in any of those extremely taxing playing time decisions.

Sending Ace Junior out to play shortstop—or second base—for every inning of the season was the easiest thing that Ace had to do all year long.

Thankfully, that's one place where Ace felt absolutely no pressure. None whatsoever.

If only they all could be like Ace Junior.

Tens of millions of kids have played Little League baseball since its inception. It may even be hundreds of millions world-wide.

I know that I've given arithmetic examples a couple times before, but this one will be eye-opening.

I am going to use the number 10,000,000—ten million—for my example. Let's establish that those ten million little ballplayers were on Little League teams during a fifty year period of time—a half-century.

Ten million kids have come out to play on hundreds of thousands of Little League teams, each of them with a twelve man roster.

Ace plays Ace Junior, and five of Junior's teammates, for every one of the innings that his team plays that season.

This means that he has six full-time players and six part-time players. Six players will always sit on the bench during every game and the other six kids will never sit on the bench during any game.

Extrapolate that out and it's pretty simple.

Fifty percent of his team has to spend part of their time on the bench. Meanwhile, the other fifty percent never sit on the bench at all.

And once Ace and his sinister pals are exposed, they have no basis for a defense other than to tell you that they are the Head Coach, and they know what they're doing.

What they base that thinking on is known only to them.

And, unfortunately, the number of Ace-related benchwarmers is much higher than five million. In reality, there are tens of millions of them.

Fifty percent is the number that I'm trying to highlight here— HALF OF THE KIDS!

This is an epidemic that has been allowed to fester and it's time for it to stop.

You can't put lipstick on a pig.

And that lipstick doesn't work anymore in Hackensack and Flint and Honolulu and Montpelier and Marietta...

One weekend nearly fifty years ago, a Navy buddy and I drove from San Diego to Los Angeles to watch the Red Sox play the Angels in a weekend series.

Friday night's game turned out to be amazing, as we were treated to a matchup featuring two of the greatest pitchers of their era—Nolan Ryan and Luis Tiant!

Both pitchers were mowing 'em down all night and the Red Sox were trailing 3-1 in the top of the ninth. They got a runner on base and my childhood hero, Carl Yastrzemski, came up to bat. And he smashed a home run right over our heads in the bleachers and the ball game was all tied up! WOW!

In the 15th inning, the Angels finally broke through and scored the winning run. It was a night of outstanding baseball, and we were thrilled to have been able to watch it in person. The Red Sox lost, but it was a great game.

During that game, the Red Sox had a rookie in their lineup named Cecil Cooper. Time after time, Cooper came to the plate and he just kept striking out.

He struck out six times that night. Six times in one game!

On Saturday afternoon, we got there nice and early because it was Bat Day and we wanted to make sure that we got one. There were only a handful of fans in the park at that early hour, so we wound up right down by the Red Sox dugout talking with outfielder Juan Beniquez.

He told us stories and answered our questions and it felt very comfortable. It was so relaxed that I felt the urge to tell Beniquez exactly what I thought of young Mr. Cooper's performance from the night before.

Basically, I asked Beniquez what in the heck the Red Sox were thinking about when they inserted Cecil Cooper into a big-league lineup.

I figured that my extensive knowledge of baseball would qualify me to make such a bold assessment, and then say it out loud.

Juan Beniquez had a totally different opinion than mine. He told me, in no uncertain terms, that Cooper was going to be an excellent hitter and an outstanding ballplayer.

And later that same afternoon, Cecil Cooper belted three doubles and two singles. He pulverized the baseball all game long.

Cecil Cooper would go on to smash more than 2,000 big league career hits along with more than 200 home runs.

He had a career batting average of .298, which happens to be higher than dozens of Hall of Famers. He was a star in Major League Baseball for many years.

And I was COMPLETELY WRONG! I was ready to put him on the bench for good after watching him play in just one game!

We are often *prisoners of the moment*. I remember one time when I watched a rookie named Steve Lyons blast two homers for the Red Sox in a game in late May. He tore the cover off the ball that night.

The next morning, I was on-the-air singing his praises, as if he were going to challenge baseball's All-Time home run record.

Lyons went on to become a solid major leaguer for nine years, but he only hit a grand total of 19 career home runs. That's an average of just TWO homers per season!

I've made similar terrible talent assessment mistakes all my life.

I wonder if it would be possible for me to make those same type of errors while measuring the talent of an eleven-year-old?

My first exposure to organized baseball was in Farm League.

I was only nine during that first season, but I'd been playing games with older kids for years. And I knew that I was more than ready to play when I finally got out there on a baseball diamond for real.

When I pitched, I overpowered them. When I was hitting, it was a mismatch. It was no more than glorified batting practice. Most of the other kids were just getting indoctrinated into the sport, whereas I'd been immersed in it for years.

Baseball had been my top priority ever since I was four years old. It made perfect sense that I would be miles ahead of the other kids in the league.

It wasn't long before I was promoted up to Little League, right in the middle of the season.

I jumped at the chance to play against the bigger kids and the better competition. I was going to be the youngest player in the league, and also one of its tiniest. But I was all fired-up and couldn't wait.

In Farm League, I was on the Cubs. That meant that I had a navy-blue T-shirt with CUBS written on the front. We wore blue jeans and sneakers. And we got a blue cap with a red C on it. That was it.

In Little League, I was on the Phillies. We had matching red pinstriped shirts and pants. We had stirrups to go over our socks. And we got to wear little spikes too! It was a big change. For a little guy, it felt like I was in the big leagues!

The coach sent me out to right field for the first game. I hadn't even met him before I got to the field that day. He took one look at me and put me in the outfield. I am sure that my size factored into his decision.

You can go to any Little League field and watch the coach hitting infield practice. He sends four infielders out there and three of his outfielders too.

He hits a grounder to the third baseman and tells the kid to throw the ball to first. Next he moves on to the shortstop, and then the second baseman. Lather. Rinse. Repeat.

It usually ends up with a pile of errors, and it never goes as smoothly as Ace wants it to go. Then, right at the end, he tries to hit one fly ball to each one of the outfielders.

On its face, it is a useless, time-wasting drill. But every Ace, in every state, does it the same mindless way before every game. They do that because it's the only way they've ever seen it done before.

Snore.

You already know how much I love baseball—watching it, listening to it, playing it, analyzing it, and learning about it.

So instead of day-dreaming in the outfield during infield practice, I was watching my new teammates like a hawk.

One thing I noticed right away was that our shortstop kept throwing the ball much too high, and far too wide to the right of our first baseman.

The first baseman would lunge as far as he could, but he would still be unable to get any leather on the ball. Thus, it would sail past him and roll all the way to the fence every time.

And that shortstop continued to make the same off-target tosses every time that he was told to throw the ball to first base.

Sure enough, the first batter of the game hit a ground ball right at that shortstop. The kid picked it up and guess what? Grin!

It must have been muscle memory because the ball again sailed high, and well wide to the right of the first baseman. It wasn't a big surprise to me.

But this time, that baseball didn't roll all the way to the fence. And that was true because I had roared in from right field, and picked it up before it even got close to that fence.

Then I whirled around and fired the ball to the second baseman, who easily tagged the runner, who was out by the proverbial mile!

My cap had fallen off while I was running in to retrieve the ball, so I had to go back and get it. A man who was standing near the fence picked it up and handed it back to me.

As he did, he patted me on the head and excitedly said,

"That's why the Phillies win ballgames, young man, that's why the Phillies win ballgames!"

Huh?

I was only nine years old and he was probably thirty-nine, for all I knew, but what he had just said didn't make one lick of sense.

This guy apparently was making this curious observation as if I were part of some longstanding winning tradition that made the Phillies the gold standard for Little League teams around that town!

It was utterly ridiculous considering the fact that I didn't even know the names of that shortstop, the first baseman, or any other Phillies on my team for that matter!

I didn't know any them.

That's why the Phillies win ballgames?

I don't even know if this ever happens any more.

Every summer morning, not long after the rooster sounded off, my mother would put a peanut butter and jelly sandwich and a bag of chips into a brown paper bag.

Then she'd give me a dime to buy a Coke to wash down my lunch, and I'd head off to play baseball all day long and well into the night!

Imagine that?

Is there anything like that going on in your neighborhood these days?

I realize that I'm talking about a bygone era, but man it was SO much fun!

The *Boys of Summer*?

You bet your life we were!

It could be raining cats and dogs, and we'd still be out there loving life.

Nobody needed to call one another to set things up either. It was as if we were required to be there, almost like showing up for school in other parts of the year.

We would play ten games a day, maybe even more. We certainly weren't keeping track. We started about eight in the morning and didn't get back to our houses until the sun had gone down.

We were playing for the love of the game!

We chose two captains and they would try to make sure that the teams were as evenly-matched as possible.

One of the captains would pick the first player—the one that he determined to be the *best of the best*. And then the other captain would get the chance to choose the next two *best* kids.

From there, it alternated until all of our names were called.

On the very first day that first summer, I got picked last, entirely due to my age and my size. And that probably became the first *goal* I ever set for myself—to not get picked last!

For a couple days, I did get picked last, but I was a darn good little ballplayer who got lots and lots of hits, and I could run faster than almost all of them too.

By the end of the week, I was already being chosen in the middle of the pack. I was playing with the big boys and I was more than holding my own.

But what if Ace had been my coach on the first day of that summer? He would have no doubt picked me last too. And when

Ace picks you last, nothing good is gonna happen for you after that.

And you already know that my supposed lack of talent would be the exact reason that I would've never seen the light of day. I was destined to be sitting on Ace's bench.

He'd see absolutely no future for me in his plans, and then simply continue on with his Little League championship chasing ways.

My opportunity to play baseball would have disappeared into the ether, and be gone forever.

I'm not naive enough to believe that all Little League coaches will have the stomach, the inner fortitude, to put their little Ace Junior on the bench for a game or two.

But the ones who do put Junior on the bench for the very first time in his life will find that it actually feels quite refreshing for them to do so!

Ace would finally realize that it's not the end of the world.

Next, he'll start recognizing that he has new favorite players on his own team! Once he gets a glimpse beyond the blinders that came with trying to make Ace Junior the great ballplayer that Ace so badly wanted him to become, Ace begins to see the bigger picture.

It makes the universe sing with how wonderful it is for the ones who can make this simple adjustment.

Yet sadly, we are never going to run out of Aces who can read these stories and STILL not be able to put Ace Junior on the bench for even one inning.

I knew a guy named Mike from Karaoke Night at a club in our town.

He was a quiet, introspective man who absolutely loved music. He told me he had a guitar, and I believe he owned a set of drums too.

Mike would strum his fingers softly on the bar, and sing almost every song quietly to himself. He frequently sat alone and didn't seem to mind.

During the time that I knew Mike, I had a really cool segment on my Friday night sports talk show. I had created my own special version of *Open Mike Night,* and made it available to everybody in town.

On my Friday morning sportscasts, I'd tell the listeners that I'd be showing up in a stretch limousine at Frankie's Pizza and Millie's Coffee Shop and Freddie's Jewelry and Bill's Car Wash and Gertie's Bridal Shop and so forth.

I invited members of my audience to come and visit me at any of that week's locations. And everybody knew that I'd be spending just five minutes at each establishment. We even had a countdown timer!

Be there or be square! Time was of the essence. It was great exposure for the businesses, the listeners loved it, and so did I.

I'd have a fresh topic every week. The best NFL team of all time. The greatest rebounder in basketball. The toughest boxer ever and so on. So if they wanted to chime in, I'd tape record their responses at the various places, and play them back on my show later that night.

It came as quite a surprise for me to see Mike waiting for me when our limo pulled up at Jenny's Bakery one Friday afternoon.

That week's topic was for my listeners to summon their Best *Childhood Sports Memory,* and Mike sure looked *locked and loaded* and ready to party!

It was completely out of character to see how eager he was to participate. I was more than a little bit interested in what he planned on telling me.

He'd normally speak in a low monotone whenever I'd see him. He was simply not an excitable boy. But when I put that microphone in front of him on that Friday afternoon, he lit up like a Christmas tree!

"Jake, I can remember back when I played Little League baseball. I was NOT a good ballplayer. The coach had me sitting on the bench all season long."

"But in the championship game, I came up to bat with the other team ahead by two runs, and the bases were loaded. And I hit a home run right over the center field fence! I hit a grand slam to win the championship for us that day, and it might have been the best moment of my life!"

And the reason Mike believed that he wasn't a good ballplayer was because Ace created the false narrative by having Mike just sit and rot on his bench.

By the way, on that Friday night, I opened my show with Mike's story.

And later, I closed the show with Mike's story again!

I just wanted to give Ace two chances to be listening.

"There is a vitality, a life force, an energy, a quickening that is translated through you into action, and because there is only one of you in all time, this expression is unique. And if you block it, it will never exist through any other medium and will be lost."
– Martha Graham

And every day I wonder why Ace insists on blocking little kids, and doing it with such wanton disregard.

What enormous power he wields, huh?

And he'll be wielding it again tonight in Sacramento and Chandler and Olongapo and Topeka and Coral Gables...

"A coach will impact more people in one year than the average person does in a lifetime." – Billy Graham

Did you ever wake up feeling like you are Mr. Big Stuff?

Maybe you spend part of your time believing that you're the reason that the world turns on its axis in the manner that it does.

Ace feels exactly this way on all matters as they pertain to his Little League team.

I have a thought on that subject.

Many years ago, when ships were wood and men were iron, I served onboard an amphibious Navy ship. We were the flagship for our task force. I was the lead communicator, who was responsible for all the radio and communications circuits for each of the five ships in the Squadron.

Our ship made voyages to the Mediterranean, the Caribbean, the North Atlantic and beyond. For four years, that ship was my home address. If you couldn't reach me with a message in a bottle, you had to send my mail to a Fleet Post Office.

During that time, we won lots of communications awards. And I was personally decorated for my work. And it was my distinct pleasure to have the opportunity to do it.

It was good work, and it was important work too.

But all good things must come to an end because my active duty service was nearing its exciting conclusion.

When you are getting close to waving goodbye, the crew starts calling you a *short timer*! It was time for me to start enjoying civilian life again.

Our ship was scheduled to go out on another six-month cruise to the Mediterranean Sea, about a month after I was scheduled to ship out.

In the Radio Shack, crew members began wondering who would be taking my place because I had been in charge for so long.

About that same time, we had a new Chief Petty Officer come aboard to take over our department. He was going to be in charge of the Radio Shack for the upcoming cruise.

That Chief had spent fifteen years in the Navy, but somehow had only served one year aboard ship during all that time. Now his mission was to lead all communications for a flagship preparing for a Mediterranean cruise, and he had very little experience to draw upon.

One day, he called me into his office and made me this proposition,

"Jake, I don't want you to get out of the Navy right now. I am asking you to extend your tour of duty by six months."

"And if you'll come on this cruise with us, I'm prepared to offer you $5000 cash if you agree to do it. When the ship pulls into any port, you can head out as soon as the gangway goes down, and you wouldn't have to come back until we're ready to shove off again. Whaddya say?"

I was only earning around $1000 a month in those days, so $5000 cash would be like having another five months of pay all at once.

The extra time off in Spain and Italy and France and Greece and Sicily would've been a nice bonus too. But it was time for me to head on home.

That Chief made me feel indispensable that night. But I didn't take him up on his offer.

And guess what?

One month later, my *former* ship sailed from Norfolk, Virginia to Rota, Spain, and began their six-month odyssey without me.

And they did just fine! None of us is indispensable.

This is a long way around to informing you that your Little League lineup would be fare just as well without Ace Junior right in the middle of it for every inning of every game!

Allow me to be interactive with you here for a moment or two.

Let's have some fun!

Stand in front of a mirror with your feet spread about shoulder width apart.

Position yourself so that your back is facing toward home plate and pretend that you are receiving an imaginary throw from an outfielder.

Pantomime catching the ball and getting ready to spin around to make a relay throw, either to home plate, or to one of the other bases behind you.

If you are right handed, I want you to plant your right foot on the ground and turn gracefully to your left, so you can locate your imaginary target, and then make your throwing motion.

Do it two or three times and you will develop a rhythm. It'll feel smooth and natural, and it's gonna feel that way because it's the right way to do it.

Now start over in the same position. Receive the imaginary throw. But this time, plant your left foot and turn to your right, while you are trying to locate the imaginary target.

You'll see that there's NOTHING graceful about it at all, when you turn to your right, especially when you compare it to how natural and comfortable you felt when you turned to your left!

Plus, you'd end up having to adjust your feet with two, three or even four little crow hop steps, just to get yourself back on solid footing, before you can even think about making your throw toward the target.

Turning the wrong way completely robs you of your balance. It's even possible that you could stumble, and possibly even fall down!

Now watch a big-league ballgame tonight, and you'll see major league baseball players turning the wrong way when they accept the throws that come in from the outfield.

Observe the shortstops and second basemen as they grab the throws from the outfielders. Crazy as it sounds, sometimes they turn the wrong way!

It's not debatable. They are doing it backwards!

And once you become aware of this, and begin to watch for it, you'll laugh every single time you see one of them do it. It is just plain lazy, and it's inexplicable that a coaching staff would ever allow it to happen, even once!

Every Little Leaguer that I coached understands how to do it properly, and they'll remember how to do it correctly for the rest of their lives. I taught them how to do it the right way, and the wrong way, and it's a lesson they'll never forget.

You can't teach a kid to be a freak of nature like Bo Jackson or

Mike Trout or Mickey Mantle, but you can teach him how to do the little things properly.

And then you gotta LET HIM PLAY so he can have the chance to do the things you taught him!

Who's the biggest, smartest, fastest, oldest, wisest?

I remember working as a young sportswriter covering a local high school football team. They'd won 21 straight ballgames—including a state championship—and they continued to run roughshod over every team that had visions of halting their long streak of victories.

One Saturday afternoon, they had a game about fifty miles away against a small school from a rural community. The two teams had never met in their history. Half of the team had never even heard of the town where the school was located.

Everyone figured it would be an easy win, and they expected their victory train to just keep chugging along.

And it did turn out to be an easy win.

The kids who lived up in those woods bushwhacked the kids from our town that afternoon! I'm not much at remembering scores, but they won the game by at least three touchdowns. It was a slobber knocker!

It was a huge upset. It was remarkable. It was amazing. It was incomprehensible. Believe me, it was all those things and more.

The king was knocked completely off his throne that day, and then he was taken out behind the woodshed. What else goes on in those woods?

And who knows what other secrets haven't been revealed in unexpected places?

One of life's unmistakable lessons is to realize that there is always gonna be somebody bigger and badder than you.

Maybe that little kid sitting on your bench is a lot bigger and badder than you will ever know.

Maybe he's even bigger and badder than Ace Junior.

Perish the thought!

Here's one that you've undoubtedly already witnessed.

At the end of the regular season, Little League coaches get to vote for kids to play on the league All-Star team, which leads to this potential discussion,

"Hey Ace, did you vote for Ace Junior to play on the league All-Star team?"

"Of course, I did He's the best player on the team and probably the best player in the whole league!"

"Oh I see."

Maybe that's why Little League All-Star teams wind up having entire rosters chock full of little Ace Juniors playing on them!!!

Unfortunately, this happens every season in Columbus and Madison and Gilbert and San Juan and Lincoln...

When I speak to people eye-to-eye about this subject, they have no trouble understanding how important this is to me.

How seriously do I take my mission?

As I've stated previously, I stand out on the Las Vegas Strip seven days a week, all year round, talking to people about my non-stop worldwide effort to obliterate the Little League status quo.

Plus, I sure know how to draw a crowd! I'm not difficult to spot on Las Vegas Boulevard either. Folks are drawn to me. Everybody loves a Snowman!

And I believe that I'm the only Snowman here in town.

People love their baseball and they love their kids. I'm able to gain their interest and their trust quickly, and my message continues to spread like wildfire.

That's why I share with you just about every little thought that comes into my mind. I never know which one of these stories or tidbits will serve as the one that finally turns the light on for Ace.

Sometimes it probably sounds like I'm stomping my foot while I'm typing. And you're correct in thinking that way.

I need to make sure people realize that half of the kids who have ever signed up to play Little League baseball are banished to the bench by their own coaches, as if these young boys had somehow failed inspection!

It's simple math. Half of the kids sit on the bench during the season and the other half of the eleven-year-olds never have to sit and watch from the bench.

Never. Nada. Not once.

Suffice it to say, it's rampant and it's scary. And Ace gets away with it in every game, during every season, and he does it right under our noses.

Here is what I do know for sure. People learn from my words.

My thought is that if a nugget of any size happens to hit the bullseye, then there will be a kid somewhere in the world tonight who will get to play third base for the first time in his life.

That little boy will benefit due to the enlightenment of another Little League coach!

Every night I go to bed smiling, and every morning I wake up refreshed and ready to continue motivating all my friends, new and old, from all over the world to march on with me.

I love it when a community produces a major league ballplayer.

It's exciting for everybody in the city.

The little kids can climb into their beds at night and dream of one day being the town's next big star.

They know that somebody who lived right down the street from them grew up playing Little League baseball, and now they're playing in the big leagues.

Now if those tiny ballplayers could just somehow convince Ace to let them play on their own Little League teams.

Wanna hear something that sounds pompous?

I welcome opposing viewpoints, but frankly I don't see how there could be any.

What could be better than befriending, teaching, practicing, playing games and having fun with all of your Little Leaguers?

Am I ever gonna stop saying the same thing over and over?

NOPE!

Benjamin always liked throwing a baseball and, as time went by, he could throw it faster and faster.

One summer night, he was on the mound firing on all cylinders. After four innings, he still hadn't given up any hits and had already struck out ten batters.

I remember thinking that if I'd been his coach that season, he wouldn't have had a chance to strike out so many hitters. I rarely let one of my little guys pitch for more than two innings at a time.

That way I would be able to send three different pitchers to the mound in each game. There were always plenty of kids that wanted to pitch.

Ten kids had shown up for the game that night, so naturally nine of them would be on the field at once, and the other kid would sit on the bench.

Ace announced the starting lineup and everybody got to go out in the field—except for Mike. He was the only one who would have to sit in the dugout.

That wasn't the end of the world I suppose, but it became troublesome when Ace had Mike sitting in there for four innings in a row. Meanwhile every one of his teammates were playing in the ballgame.

Finally, Ace put Mike in right field for the fifth inning. But in the sixth—and final inning—he used the re-entry rule and SAT MIKE DOWN ON THE BENCH AGAIN!

Yes! That time the capital letters absolutely meant that I was HOLLERING MY HEAD OFF while I was typing that!

Benjamin was still in the process of throwing a no-hitter when he walked out to the mound for the final inning. But he never threw a pitch. He set the ball down on the pitching rubber and walked back into the dugout.

And he said to Ace,

"Coach, you just don't get it. Let Mike play and I'll sit in the dugout. As a matter of fact, why don't you let Mike pitch?"

133

Can you imagine being Ace and having an eleven-year-old kid approach you with that no-brainer logic?

And it just so happened to be a kid who was pitching a no-hitter that night!

My view on that particular verbal exchange was to look skyward, and tell God that it was OK to bring me to heaven now. My son was more than ready to carry my torch!

When I was little, we didn't call it a rundown when a player was caught between two bases. We called it a pickle.

And every Little League game seems to have lots of *pickles.* The little guys get confused on the bases and find themselves in no-man's land, not exactly sure which direction that they should run next.

It's hysterical. Mayhem ensues!

Most of the time, the runners are able to escape, and scramble themselves out of those pickles, because the kids who were trying to catch them almost always make a mistake.

The *pickle* usually features wild throws, dropped balls and plenty of confusion by the defense. Other times, the runner appears to be so fast that he can just sprint himself out of the *pickle,* before the kids who were chasing him around could get organized.

Kids throw the ball back and forth as much as they do because they believe that's what they are supposed to do. Maybe their thought is that if they make the runner keep running back and forth, then he'll eventually get tired and they can easily tag him out.

The correct way to do it is to make the runner go back to the base he just came from. You show him the ball in your throwing hand, repeatedly make little ball fakes, forcing him to run back in the direction that you want him to go.

Then when he finally makes up his mind to try and race back, you simply toss it to the player at that base who can easily apply the tag. There is nothing else you need to know when you want to catch the runner and tag him out.

We had lots of baseball drills that involved every kid on the team taking part, so that we all could learn together. One of those drills was teaching them what to do if they got another kid caught between the bases.

We did it at almost every practice because it taught the kids to run and throw and catch and hustle and think and execute. And every one of them could do it perfectly by the end of the season!

It was so cool to be their coach, and watch them put their new skills into action during the games. They were like a vice in a way because if you got trapped in a pickle with my little guys, you weren't going to escape from it!

They did it surgically! It was a beautiful thing.

Youngsters can learn anything when you take the time to teach them.

All of them.

When I got out of the Navy, I played small college hoops.

We were an excellent team, and not just on the scoreboard. We got along famously. I remember how we roamed throughout the Midwest, riding on buses just about every weekend, to get to our games!

Some of those trips were a four-hour drive from our campus.

Yet despite covering all that territory to reach our faraway destinations, normally there wouldn't be more than a hundred fans in the stands to watch us play. We basically toiled in obscurity.

Every Snow Often, one of my teammates would wistfully wonder aloud about how we practiced so hard and played so well, but nobody else seemed to care about us.

Somehow that made me think about those Little League *travel teams*. Carloads of Ace's kids get up at five o'clock in the morning, and drive to another city, so they could play the *supposedly elite ballplayers* from another town which, of course, is nothing more than another roster full of Ace's kids.

More than ninety percent of the players in Little League never have a chance to play on a *travel team*. We already know that some youngsters don't even get the opportunity to play on their own teams!

I've got an idea on this too. This could be so much fun.

Here's what I propose:

At the end of the regular season, we would have a league-wide celebration for all the players and coaches. It would be a day loaded with fun and food and drinks and games and prizes.

And everyone would be eagerly anticipating the day's *Main Event*.

We'd put the names of every kid in the league into a hat, and have twenty four names drawn. And those lucky kids would be the ones to play on the travel teams!

The first twelve would be on *Team #1* and the next dozen would play for *Team #2*.

And we could do that in Cheyenne and Allentown and Rancho Cucamonga and Bettendorf and Winter Haven...

Why not?

"7-8-9!, 7-8-9!"

The Little League scorekeeper calls that out in a loud voice between innings.

The inference is that it should be an easy inning for the pitcher, because supposedly the worst players on the team would be batting 7th or 8th or 9th—the final three spots in the batting order.

Not on my team they didn't. Our little guys batted in the order that they showed up to play for us that night.

And I made sure that every one of our players had a chance to bat in every spot in the batting order during the season.

Ours was an equal opportunity team.

Besides, we didn't have any WORST players!

Our cutoff drills were every bit as much fun as our pickle drills.

Practicing the relay plays helped us in so many ways. Every kid would know the arm strength and accuracy for every one of his teammates who would be throwing the ball back into the infield.

This helped each player to realize that sometimes he might have to run a little further into the outfield to accept the throws from the different outfielders.

If the ball doesn't hit the ground, defensive plays tend to be crisper and the ball will get to its final destination faster.

We called it *Help a Teammate Day*.

We would station half of the kids in the outfield and the rest of them would be deployed around the infield. The players in the infield would have their backs towards home plate facing the kids in the outfield.

Then I would hit the ball past one of the outfielders, who would have to run to catch up with it, and then he'd have to turn and fire the baseball back into the infield.

But where should he throw it? How would he know?

He'd know right away where to throw it, because I would tell one of the kids in the infield to repeatedly call out the outfielder's name as loudly as he could.

This helped because when the outfielder turned around to make his throw, he'd know exactly where to throw it since he had received such perfect audio directions from his infielder.

Plus the infielder would be waving his arms—crossing them furiously back and forth high over his head—in order to give his teammate a beautiful visual target making it very easy for him to spot too!

Naturally, I'd choose a different outfielder and infielder for every new play and rotated all the kids through both positions.

Again this exercise included throwing, running, catching, thinking, executing, and having a great time. They now knew the importance of relays, where and when to throw the ball, and they'd all keep improving their footwork in the process—all of that in one simple drill!

It also encouraged togetherness, camaraderie and fun.

We got better every time we got together, whether we were practicing or playing in a game.

Do you have a favorite kid? Do you like one kid more than another one?

On my team, they were all my favorites.

But there was one kid named Philip, and I know that I developed an extra soft spot in my heart for him.

His father had died during the previous winter, and Philip and his mom were trudging through life trying to make sense of it all. I didn't know him before the season and had no idea what he was like beforehand, but I could see a distinct sadness in his eyes.

His mom had a beautiful spirit, and she told me several times how good it was for Philip to play on our particular team.

Philip was the fastest runner that we had on our team. It was pure God-given speed. He didn't make a big deal of it, but when he was in the outfield, and somebody hit the baseball into the gap, he would track it down faster than anybody in the league.

And he was a good kid in all facets of his personality too.

I remember one time when he took a pack of gum from his pocket, and asked if anybody wanted a piece. He gave out one stick at a time to everybody who asked for one. I noticed that his pack was empty, and he hadn't even kept one for himself!

How cool was that?!

As I've written a number of times, everybody on my team got a chance to play ALL the positions that they wanted to play. There were no exceptions. If you wanted to be a shortstop at some point, all you had to do was tell me and you'd play shortstop.

I say *no exceptions*, but that's not a complete truism.

If a kid told me that he wanted to pitch, I'd make extra darn sure that he had the arm strength to reach home plate consistently. He'd also need to be able to throw enough strikes to be competitive.

What I didn't want was for the little guy to become embarrassed, which obviously would have been the case, if his pitches weren't reaching home plate.

That would defeat the whole purpose! I made sure they realized that was the only reason I did it that way.

I didn't care if a kid gave up eight home runs in a row. I just wanted to watch him pitch!

Looking back, every kid who wanted to pitch for us wound up on the pitching mound during the season.

Why was I so adamant about this aspect of coaching? Well, the way I had it figured was that if the kids weren't allowed to pitch or play shortstop or center field or catcher when they were little guys, who was going to let them play those positions once they got older?

Ace's idiotic methods made absolutely sure that his benchwarmers would have no experience at any position!

Go to any ball field anywhere, and you'll hear a little apple-cheeked kid telling you that he's a third baseman. He says that because Ace foolishly pigeon-holes his Little Leaguers into one specific defensive position, as if he is a big-league manager.

Think about that. Ace installs an 11-year-old boy as his third baseman, and then sets it up so that no other kid would play third base for his team that season.

Could anything be stupider?

Ace then puts his *inferior players*, the ones he begrudgingly plays for one inning in each game, out in right field.

Then when a ball is hit out to right field, which is actually the most difficult defensive position on the field to play, Ace gets all upset when his *benchwarmer* misses the ball and can't make the play cleanly.

I'm not kidding! And all of these things are gonna happen again tonight in Saratoga and Chattanooga and Wilkes-Barre and Rock Island and Littleton...

It's rampant and it MUST BE STOPPED!

Ace truly feels as if he is doing everything the right way. He is just doing what he's seen before. It is ridiculous, but these guys feel as if they have the recipe for success, which of course begins and ends with their sheer nepotism.

Let me get back to Philip. He spoke very rarely, but he did ask me one night if I would really let him pitch if he wanted to do it. I told him that it would be my pleasure.

Twice I asked him if he was ready to pitch in the following inning. Both times he said, "*Thanks Coach, maybe next time...* "

Finally, *next time* came, and I sent him out to the mound for the fourth inning. I couldn't wait to watch him pitch! I thoroughly enjoyed seeing his eyes, his enthusiasm, his smile.

Philip walked the first three batters he faced. He was throwing hard, and he was enjoying himself. But he just couldn't get the baseball to cooperate.

I went to the mound to see if he wanted to keep trying to find the strike zone.

He looked at me and said, "*Coach, I am loving this. Can I stay out here?*" I gave him a pat and told him he could stay out there all afternoon if he wanted!

He walked the next batter and then hit the next kid with a pitch. And it didn't deter him one bit. He looked at me anxiously wondering if I was going to take him out. And I didn't move an inch.

The next kid hit the ball right back to the mound, and Philip started a double play. It was a beautiful thing. He struck out the next kid on three pitches, and you would have thought he won the World Series.

When he came back to the bench, it was as if he was a different kid altogether. And guess who pitched the next two innings? And you should have seen how happy he was after he struck out six of the last seven batters that he faced. Three innings pitched, no hits allowed!

After the game, a parent of one of the kids on the opposing team said to me, "*You are lucky that Philip started throwing strikes. It's almost like you don't even care if you deny the other kids on your team a chance to win the game.*"

I looked at the woman and said, "*Well, let's examine your thought. I would prefer to think of it as me not denying Philip a chance to pitch.*"

That's all the time I had for her. It was time to go and enjoy ice cream cones with the kids. And the whole time that I was licking mine, I was watching Philip who maybe, just maybe, had his best day ever!

How would I know if I was putting the next global superstar on the mound that night? How would I ever know if I didn't let him try it?

A nine-year-old kid looked up at me one day and said,

"Mr. Snow, I want to be a Minor League Ballplayer."

Why in heaven's name would a kid ever even entertain a thought like that?

My educated guess was that he was on a Little League team and didn't get to play very much. So he figured that he probably wasn't going to be good enough to play in the Major Leagues.

And I bet he thought about things like that a lot while he was sitting on Ace's bench.

I can't imagine any other explanation . Can you?

Let's go ask Ace what his thoughts are on the matter.

There are a lot of Little League coaches who are clairvoyant!

They can foresee the future with pinpoint accuracy. On the first day that they assume their roles as a Little League head coach, they are absolutely certain about what's gonna happen next!

Can you imagine that?!

They are positive about what is gonna transpire. It's cut and dried. They know they're right. They can feel it deep down in their bones. They were never surer about anything else in their whole lives.

Every new coach has the same magical powers.

They are able to operate with this supreme confidence because they know, without a shadow of a doubt, that Ace Junior is going to play a specific position on defense, have a permanent spot in the batting order, and will also be playing in the Little League All-Star game later on in the summer!

And you can watch Ace Junior play in those All-Star games in Pine Bluff and Harper's Ferry and Sochi and Essex Junction and Davenport...

More than once, I've had a Little Leaguer tell me what he was,

"I'm a pitcher."

"Cool! Do you like to pitch? Can you throw the ball really fast?"

"I'm a second baseman."

"Great! You must like fielding ground balls and catching popups."

"I'm a benchwarmer."

"Wow! You must really enjoy sitting in the dugout watching all the other kids play baseball."

Five Little League moms are sitting on the bleachers cheering for their team.

Four of the moms have sons who play in every inning of every game. The fifth mom has a son who sits in the dugout for four or five innings every night.

The conversation is friendly. They're having a nice time. They've become friends because they see one another at all the games.

When one of the mom's son comes up to bat, she stops the conversation for a minute and watches him hit. She cheers for her boy and then returns to their conversation.

And that's how it goes. Each mom takes a turn watching her son in the batter's box.

The fifth mom doesn't have to interrupt the conversation very often because her son doesn't get his turn at the plate until the final inning.

Can you imagine how much fun she has at the game?

And her job might just be starting, because she will probably need to console a sad little boy when they get home.

Have you ever heard the story about Walter Mitty?

Walter is a character from the imagination of author James Thurber. To me, it's a story about a dreamer and I root for anyone that has a vision that makes them have a continuous zest for life!

I haven't read *The Secret Life of Walter Mitty* in a long time. But I remember what happened when he would go to the grocery store with his wife.

She would firmly instruct him to stay in the car, and not go anywhere, until he saw her coming out with the groceries. There was very little doubt about who was in charge of the whole operation in the Mitty household.

But once she left, Walter would sit there holding the steering wheel pretending to be a famous fighter pilot or else he would morph into one of a million other vibrant characters that would make him feel strong and important.

He was a dreamer and he was good at it!

And on every Little League bench, every night of the week, there are benchwarmers who are sitting there dreaming of one day being a big-league ballplayer.

Daniel Nava was a little guy who had big dreams too.

Daniel was a kid who weighed only 84 pounds as a freshman in high school. He was constantly fighting against the prejudices he encountered due to his size.

Later on down the line, he was a walk-on—a non-scholarship player—for the Santa Clara college baseball team. But he was subsequently cut from the squad and didn't get a chance to play that year.

Nava spent that season as the team's equipment manager. He washed their uniforms instead of playing baseball with them.

On every step of his path, Daniel Nava was told by coaches and others that he was too short, too skinny, and simply too small.

But he wanted to play so badly, and he wasn't about to discard his dream!

After college, he played in the Golden Baseball Independent League and, incredibly, led the league in hitting with a .371 batting average!

That's when the Boston Red Sox swooped down and signed him to a contract for $1.

Yes, one dollar!

And during the very next season, Daniel Nava was called up to the major leagues! He went from washing underwear and socks for his college team to playing first base for the Boston Red Sox!

And what do you think was the first thing that Daniel did once he got to Fenway Park?

Daniel Nava stepped up to home plate, in front of a capacity crowd, and smashed a grand slam home run on the very first pitch he ever saw in the big leagues!

True story.

Just out of curiosity, Ace, if he was 84 pounds as a freshman in High School, how big do you think he was in Little League?

I bet you would have had a special spot all picked out for him right at the end of your bench.

Ace looks over his new crop of players and immediately begins the process of mentally slotting them into the positions that would help propel his Little League team to the Promised Land.

Ace sees one little guy out on the field, and decides right away that little Billy wouldn't be factoring into the team's plans for that season.

So Ace says to the kid, "*Billy, you're a little too small right now. But I'll keep you on my team and you can sit on the bench most of this year. That way you can watch the other kids and they will be teaching you how to play.* "

So Billy sits on the bench for the whole season. Can you even begin to imagine how much Billy was able to learn by watching other ten-year-olds playing baseball?!

Absurd!

Unfortunately, Billy gets Ace for his coach again the next season and, not surprisingly, his coach makes the same hurtful decision, "*Billy, you're a little bigger now, but still not big enough to help us win this year.* "

So Billy sits again, playing in only one inning per game, while getting just one measly at-bat.

When the third year rolls around, Ace tells his assistant coach, *"Billy isn't getting any better. This is his third season with us and he really hasn't gotten any better at all."*

Atta boy, Ace. Atta boy. You are ridiculous.

Utterly ridiculous.

And these nonsensical thought processes are very easy to spot in Roanoke and Corvallis and Kalamazoo and Utica and Cedar Rapids...

There he is. Your little boy is in his crib.

He's wearing a little baseball onesie. He's got a whiffle ball in there and a big plastic bat too.

You teach him how to swing it and then hoot and holler like a banshee when he smacks the ball around the floor with his bat. He likes the reinforcement that you're giving him, so he hits it again and again.

Then the next time you have company over, you show them what your little slugger can do. They clap and whistle and smile at your little prodigy.

Ace Junior continues to hit that little plastic ball until you are completely convinced that something awfully special is going on with your toddler. This could be the start of something huge.

You know that you had better coach him because you're gonna need to keep a close eye on his development. Junior is most certainly one of a kind.

I wonder if there might be any other toddlers in town, who have been dominating their households with their little plastic bats and balls too.

And those whiffle bats and balls are on sale in Pueblo and Winooski and Malibu and Plano and Hilton Head Island...

There's a table full of Little League baseball players eating their lunch at school.

They have a game that night and they're excited. One kid tells a story about the home run he hit in the last game. Another one talks about how he struck out the best player on the other team.

Everybody is weighing in, talking about one play or another.

Suddenly they notice Larry who is on their team also. Larry isn't telling any stories. He hasn't really gotten a chance to play much yet.

"Oh look, it's Larry, one of our benchwarmers. I don't even know why you keep coming. You're not good enough to play with us. You're just a benchwarmer."

Larry is only nine-years-old! And he's being tormented by a bunch of kids who play on his OWN baseball team! There probably couldn't be anything worse that could happen to a third grader.

He doesn't like being bullied. Why would he? And, even worse, he's being taunted just because he wants to play baseball!

This is where I can interject that one of the kids—usually the loudest one—is Ace Junior!

And this would be the perfect time for somebody to make Junior aware of an expression that he probably has never heard before,

"He was born on third base and thought he had hit a triple."

Ace Junior is in the lineup for the whole game, every night, and he believes he's there based upon his own merit. But our little benchwarmer is never in the lineup and has no idea why.

It's gotta be awfully confusing, and very upsetting, for the little guy.

Somehow Ace completely overlooks that kid the same way he is overlooked in Garden City and Naples and Kingman and Milwaukee and Carlsbad...

Every day I watch lots of different sports on television.

I really enjoy my teams and the games they play.

Sometimes, I'll see a fly ball that wasn't caught and say to myself, *"I would have caught that ball easily. I was very good at chasing down balls in the outfield."*

When a player swings and misses at a fastball, I'll be thinking, "*He tried to pull that pitch. I would have shortened my swing and slapped the ball into right field instead."*

I've played the games—tons of them—so I have plenty of first-hand knowledge about what a player could, and should, do on various plays throughout the game.

There are other guys in town who love the games just as much as I do. And they watch them every night too.

But they don't really have the same point of reference that I enjoy.

This is true because these other guys were benchwarmers in Little League. They signed up to play, but wound up being stymied by

Ace's careless and devastating decisions on who plays and who sits.

These guys didn't get to play when they were little, so when they watch the games now, they can't really plug themselves into the batter's box, or onto the pitching mound, or any other position on the diamond for that matter.

Ace is out there somewhere, and we know that he deserves a great big pat on the back for that. No doubt.

And Ace has inflicted these scars in Whittier and Council Bluffs and Somerset and Eau Claire and Jefferson City...

Alright Ace, here's another thought.

Let's see if we can establish some common ground here, a jumping off point, as it were.

Can we agree that the qualifications for coaching a Little League team are just about as stringent as coaching a pick-up game at the family reunion every August?

That would be fair, wouldn't it? In reality, it's exactly the same because both are unpaid volunteer positions. There are zero credentials required for either person.

Next point. Would it make any sense if you told people that you are a championship coach because you won a Little League title?

Heck, you could show them your trophy! Then you could tell them stories that would reveal the inner workings of a shrewd operation headed up by a brilliant tactician and strategist.

Do you know what I think would be more refreshing?

Let's say that, at the first practice of the season, there was one specific youngster who displayed the least amount of ability and athleticism on the field.

If you truly want to experience the really cool impact of coaching, try setting your sights on making that kid one of your favorite ballplayers.

Instead of immediately slotting him into the benchwarmer role, that you've already mentally created for him, use your time to build him up and watch him grow!

You'll love doing that and soon you'll come to realize how good it feels to do that, because you will have discovered the true beauty of coaching.

Great stuff can happen on a Little League field. Many lessons are waiting to be taught—and learned.

Teach the right ones, Ace!

And feel free to teach them in Branson and Paramus and Amherst and Bowman and Gulfport...

Did you know that more than forty percent of Americans will never move out of their original area codes?

I find this 40% number to be equally fascinating–and revealing.

By percentage, this means that a whole big bunch of our Little League coaches have never left the nest.

They are Townies.

"Yup, I live in the same house I grew up in. Grampa was a Little League coach and so was my dad. Now it's my turn. It's a family tradition."

Guess what ends up happening?

No new blood. No fresh ideas. No changes ever get made.

"We've always done it this way before."

Well, I guess that makes perfect sense then. Not!

And it doesn't make any sense in Groton and Dunedin and Wilkes-Barre and Ottumwa and Culver City...

151

My whole team stood on the baseball field with a high level of confidence.

Let me tell you why I say that.

It's because they knew that there were parts of their game, on defense, that they could do better than any other team in the league.

And the reason that they were able to feel that way was because they were completely prepared to make those particular types of plays. They knew where to go and what to do once they got there.

The key for me was not to overburden them with data and information—or a thousand little details. I've always believed that if you teach just a few fundamentals every year, it would be easily digestible for the Little Leaguers.

And in the early stages of their development, implementing *building blocks technology* works perfectly because everybody gets better and the players all root for one another.

I am convinced that if kids start at nine years old and learn just a few baseball fundamentals during each new season, they'll have *solid bricks in the wall* that will help them be prepared for when the real competition begins in high school.

I decided that our team would only work on a handful of things:

- Safety first
- Respect teammates and coaches
- Rundowns
- Relays
- Cut-Offs

And those little buggers became insanely proficient in all of those areas! I believe that was the case because they weren't bogged down with too many things cluttering up their minds.

As little as they were, they were terrific defensively.

Check this out: TEN of our twelve players played shortstop during that season. The only reason the other two kids didn't play shortstop was because they didn't want to play shortstop!

In other words, when my little guys got to the field, none of them knew where they'd be hitting in the batting order or what positions they would be playing in the field that night.

Man, we sure had a lot of fun!

Did you ever hear anyone use the word *high-handed*?

I wondered if *high-handed* was really a word. And I tried to figure out what it might mean if it actually was a real word. I thought that it might have been related to the expression *high and mighty*.

So I asked Google. And Google said,

The definition of *high-handed* is, "*Using power or authority without considering the feelings of others.*"

I've searched high and low to try and assign the exact right adjective to convey just how horribly Ace handles himself while he's on his championship-minded expedition.

And I believe that *high-handed* might just be the perfect definition to try and describe Ace's lame-brained actions.

It's a bullseye, actually. Every night, Ace proves the point that he never considers the feelings of others.

If you want to see *high-handed* behavior for yourself, all you'd have to do is visit any Little League diamond in Des Moines or Charlottesville or Wheaton or Shawnee or Decatur...

A young mother goes to every one of her son's Little League games.

The team wins most of the time, but her son doesn't get a chance to play very much baseball. All the other kids on his team play all the time.

She knows that something isn't quite right, but she doesn't really know how to approach Ace to ask for an explanation.

She doesn't want to appear as if she is whining and certainly doesn't want her son to find himself in hot water if she tries to intervene.

She just doesn't know where to find a solution.

But now, armed with this particular assortment of information and ideology, she's gonna wind up being the one who's got all the answers. And she'll be holding the hammer from this point forward!

Watch out Ace, she's gonna be coming for ya with both barrels!

And I would love to be standing there while you are stammering out your answers for the young lady. You won't have a leg to stand on and she will make sure that you realize that fact.

Be careful Ace, it's possible that she's gonna be standing and waiting for you right next to your dugout in Fairmont and Dodge City and Big Sky and Castle Rock and Fort Lauderdale...

In your zeal to coach Little Leaguers to a championship, there are going to be some things that you'll miss.

Ace, you need to know that not every kid wants to be out on the baseball field.

I remember one kid who played on my son's team. He had a really sweet left-handed batting stroke. I could tell that he was born to swing a baseball bat.

His issue was that he just didn't have the temperament to play the game of baseball. If he struck out or popped up, he'd become furious. He simply could not handle failure of any kind.

The source of his frustration could easily be traced back to his relationship with his dad. His father would scream and holler at him constantly throughout the game.

And you gotta know that those baseball conversations spilled over to the supper table and beyond.

The constant scrutiny turned out to be just too much for the kid. He flamed out in the third game of his junior year in high school. He struck out on a fastball and his father went ballistic.

The kid turned around and swore at his father. He went to the dugout, picked up his bat and glove and left the field. Forever!

He never swung a baseball bat again.

A few years later, he came to work for our radio station.

He told me that he'd always wanted to be a gymnast. He had the perfect body for it, an aptitude for it, and a burning desire to do jumps and twists and flips and spins.

But his dad insisted that he play baseball instead because,

"Baseball runs in the family!"

PSSSST, ACE!

Do you think that it's even remotely possibly that Junior isn't as much in love with baseball as you would like for him to be?

Allow yourself to give this subject a brief amount of consideration, just one quick second. Can you do that?

When you take inventory of the situation, you will begin to realize that there are other kids on your team that really did want to play and you have never gave them a chance.

Coach 'em all, Ace. That way these kinds of mistakes wouldn't happen nearly as often.

Everybody loves to have a chance for a summer getaway, maybe a week in the mountains or out at the lake.

Shumley Field was our summer getaway—a magical place where little boys gathered to play baseball every day until the sun went down.

It was one of those *"All the cool kids are doing it"* type of deals.

You could hear our bicycles, with baseball cards flapping in the tire spokes, making such a racket that it sounded like we were riding on motorcycles!

Then there were peanut butter sandwiches, friendly faces, gorgeous summer weather and the unmistakable sound of the crack of the bat!

We were just a bunch of kids ready for another day of non-stop baseball.

We did all of it by ourselves too. From organizing to lineups to scheduling to creating makeshift bases to umpiring and, come to think of it, maybe it worked out as well as it did because there were no adults around to screw it up for us.

There were no complications. We played until it was dark.

One year, a volunteer contractor built a press box at a Little League field near my home.

And he and his crew made it look awesome. It surely was pretty darn slick.

To commemorate the occasion, the league found a bunch of merchants, who were happy to give away prizes, to help celebrate the ribbon cutting ceremony. They asked me if I would come and announce the winners.

My ten-year-old daughter wanted to come along with me. She thought it was pretty cool that we were going to be the first two people ever to sit in that brand-new press box.

In the second inning, there was a close play at home plate and a runner was called out. Ace came flying out of his dugout, running toward the plate like a jackass, to begin a screaming match with a fourteen-year-old umpire.

As he walked back to his dugout, Ace turned back toward the umpire and spit as loud as a person could spit.

Sophia look at me and said, "*Yuck! That's gross, Daddy! Why is that man spitting?*"

"*I don't know sweetheart. I just don't know.*"

But Ace will be spitting again tonight in Arlington Heights and San Luis Obispo and Killington and Cape Girardeau and Valley City...

Not a day goes by without more and more of you continuing to joyfully lend your love, energy, and support!

Thank You!

One coach at a time. One team at a time. One league at a time.

And, most importantly, one kid at a time.

SnowmanLasVegas.com

Made in the USA
Columbia, SC
10 September 2022